The author of the book of Hebrews speaks of a "cloud of witnesses," heroes who actually stood their ground in trying times. Many go unnamed. Known only to God, they are nonetheless heroes, and a cloud of witnesses means they were many.

These men and women remained firm when the world pressured them otherwise. My lifelong friend, pastor Joe Champion, has written what I believe is a "for such a time as this" book. *Confronting Compromise* will encourage us to stand our ground on the eternal truth of His promises rather than giving in to the temporary pressures of this world.

Confronting Compromise is not only for Christian leaders but any believer who trusts that He is a rewarder of those who diligently seek Him.

—ROBERT BARRIGER, Founder and Senior Pastor, Camino de Vida

As ARC board members and fellow church planters, I've worked alongside and admired my friend, Joe, for a long time. He lives his life openly and authentically! What you see is what you get with him, so it's no surprise to me that he's written a practical book about how to be steadfast in your faith when those around you are falling to compromise. I wholeheartedly recommend that you take the time to let his wisdom dismantle any compromise you may have in your own life, so you can live in confidence in your relationship with God, no matter what.

—RICK BEZET, Lead Pastor, New Life Church of
Arkansas; Author, *Be Real* and *Real Love*

Confronting Compromise is full of biblical truth and personal wisdom that will empower you to stand strong, stay faithful, and walk in obedience, so you can bear much fruit for the kingdom of God.

—CHRISTINE CAINE , Best-selling Aauthor;
Founder, A21 and Propel Women

This is a book for the all-in leader. Joe Champion uses his own story and the biblical story of Eutychus to challenge leaders in every walk of life to confront compromise in their homes and hearts and on their leadership journeys. It is a must-read for any leader who is ready to go to the next level.

—HERBERT COOPER, Senior Pastor, People's
Church; Author, *But God Changes Everything*

Joe Champion's *Confronting Compromise* challenges us to keep on the pathway toward legitimate fulfillment, which God's Word promises is a treasure well worth being courageously pursued.

Compromise is a tinny substitute for the precious treasures ultimately laid up on high. Those who drift toward compromise fall short of living lives overflowing with vibrant vision. God has fixed it that way!

Joe Champion qualifies to write *Confronting Compromise* as he is unwaveringly dedicated to the vision, plan, and purposes of God and inspires others to join in!

—REV. M. D. DAVIS, President, IAM;
Founder, Pacific NW Bible College

I love the blend of wisdom and prophetic urgency Joe has woven in *Confronting Compromise*. It should be required reading for every Christian today!

—NATHAN FINOCHIO, Founder, TheosU

Choosing right doesn't always mean we get to feel right. Yet, through this brilliant story-driven book, Joe Champion teaches us how to find to the grace that overcomes the chaos. Joe is a hero of mine. I've watched him lead with joy even while walking through some of the toughest situations. His words of encouragement have resurrected my faith time and time again! Get ready to laugh and fill your heart with God's courage. *Confronting Compromise* is certain to inspire you to take on the tough problems in your world. Through a mixture of winsome story-telling and Scripture, this book will make you say: "I can do this, with God's help!" A must-read for anyone wanting to change the culture around them.

—PETER HAAS, Lead Pastor, Substance Church;
Author and Songwriter, Substance Variant

Confronting Compromise will empower you to face your fears and overcome the daily assaults on your integrity. With compelling insight into the struggles faced by leaders in the Bible, Joe Champion shares the timeless truths also evidenced by his own experiences. If you feel paralyzed by the expectations of others and pressured by cultural demands to comply, *Confronting Compromise* will set you free to be the leader God has called you to be.

—CHRIS HODGES, Senior Pastor, Church of the Highlands;
Author, *The Daniel Dilemma* and *Out of the Cave*

Have you ever found yourself in the seat of compromise? Then *Confronting Compromise* is for you. As leaders, we have to learn how to get up and confront the things that would take us away from the calling and purpose on our lives. Through biblical stories and life experience, Joe Champion will help you to find the strength to stand strong when no one else does. It's time to confront compromise!

—JOHN C. MAXWELL, Author, Speaker and Coach

In *Confronting Compromise*, Pastor Joe Champion presents tremendous insight into effectively living for Jesus every day, in the face of all kinds of challenges. With pastoral love and compassion, yet clarity, he reminds us of the value of our faith and the power of conviction and courage. It is a must-read!

—DALE O'SHIELDS, Senior Pastor, Church of
the Redeemer, Gaithersburg, Maryland

I've known Joe for many years now and *Confronting Compromise* has been burning in his heart for a long time! This is a word for the hour we are going through right now and everyone—especially leaders—needs this challenge to face the future with courage! Thank you, dear friend, for writing this book!

—DENNIS ROUSE, Founding Pastor, Victory World Church

In the Bible God asks His people over and over again, "Will you be all-in for me? Will you stop compromising?" He asks us the same questions. The life God calls us to is not one of merely trying to get by, but one of thriving. In *Confronting Compromise*, my good friend Joe Champion helps us see the incredible possibilities that are right in front of us if we are willing to stop compromising on what matters most.

—GREG SURRATT, Founding Pastor, Seacoast Church; President, ARC

Through engaging stories and reflections on biblical leadership, *Confronting Compromise* helps leaders today recognize the slippery slope of compromise and how to make decisions for fruitful, all-in lives. Christian leaders everywhere need to pick up this timely read by Joe Champion!

—DR. ROB HOSKINS, President, OneHope, Inc.

In a world of compromise, this book is *so needed* and necessary! Living above compromise is possible, but it takes what Joe Champion is teaching. I highly recommend *Confronting Compromise* for any leader in the body of Christ. No, I recommend this book for EVERY believer in the body of Christ today. We need this book more than ever, RIGHT NOW!

—MATT KELLER, Founding & Lead Pastor; Next Level Church and the Next Level Relational Network

Being a leader is not always easy. Being a Christian leader can be even more challenging. My friend Joe Champion is well acquainted with the challenges Christian leaders face and what it takes to stand for God in every area of our lives. This book will help you to have the confidence and courage to confront compromise and take your leadership to the next level!

—ROBERT MORRIS, Senior Pastor, Gateway Church; Best-selling Author of *The Blessed Life*, *Beyond Blessed*, and *Take the Day Off*

Scripture quotations marked NIV are taken from the Holy Bible, New International Version®, NIV®. Copyright © 1973, 1978, 1984, 2011 by Biblica, Inc.™ Used by permission of Zondervan. All rights reserved worldwide. www.zondervan.com. The "NIV" and "New International Version" are trademarks registered in the United States Patent and Trademark Office by Biblica, Inc.™ | Scripture quotations marked NKJV are taken from the New King James Version®. Copyright © 1982 by Thomas Nelson. Used by permission. All rights reserved. | Scripture quotations marked NLT are taken from the *Holy Bible*, New Living Translation, copyright © 1996, 2004, 2015 by Tyndale House Foundation. Used by permission of Tyndale House Publishers, Inc., Carol Stream, Illinois 60188. All rights reserved. | Scripture quotations marked MSG are taken from *THE MESSAGE*, copyright © 1993, 1994, 1995, 1996, 2000, 2001, 2002 by Eugene H. Peterson. Used by permission of NavPress. All rights reserved. Represented by Tyndale House Publishers, Inc. | Scripture quotations are from The ESV® Bible (The Holy Bible, English Standard Version®), copyright © 2001 by Crossway, a publishing ministry of Good News Publishers. Used by permission. All rights reserved. | Scripture quotations marked NASB have been taken from the (NASB®) New American Standard Bible®, Copyright © 2020 by The Lockman Foundation. Used by permission. All rights reserved. www.lockman.org

For foreign and subsidiary rights, contact the author.

ISBN: 978-1-954089-56-3   1 2 3 4 5 6 7 8 9 10

Printed in the United States of America

CONFRONTING
COMPROMISE

STAND FOR TRUTH « NO MATTER WHAT

JOE CHAMPION

AVAIL

Dedication

To my wife: Lori, the love of my life, who has led by my side for thirty years. I knew from the first time that I saw you in church that we would do life and ministry together. I am thankful that we never quit on the same day. Your heart for God and our family has given me the strength to be who God has called me to be. Thank you for never letting me sit in the seat of compromise and for loving LSU football more than I do! I love you.

To my boys: Mason, Connor, and Jackson, and to my favorite daughter, Caroline. I am so proud of who you are, and who you are becoming. Your lives remind me of God's faithfulness, and I hope the pages of this book help you as you confront compromise and stand up to be all God has called you to be. I love you.

FOREWORD

BY SAM CHAND

Some people are characters . . . and some are delightful characters. Joe Champion is in the latter category.

Pastor Joe is one of those rare "100 Percenters." Whatever he does, he does it full blast. Over the many years I've known him, I've seen his unique blend of bold vision, tender heart, and tenacity. He's fun to be around, and his wit always keeps me on my toes, because I never know what he's going to say next. It's no wonder that so many people love him and follow him!

As the pastor at Celebration Church, he has seen it grow from a mere thought through the formative years and then to incredible growth and impact. His wife, Lori, is a perfect partner—Joe is the futurist, and she puts all the pieces in place to make things happen. But don't misunderstand. It's not that he's the commander, and she's the soldier; they are equal partners in every sense of the word. Their love for and trust in each other is evident, even if you've only been with them for a few minutes.

I recall meeting with Joe and his team as we talked about the focus and strategy of growing their church and having a wider impact. Lori and the rest of the team were in the thick of things in our conversation, but Joe was sitting a bit apart reading his Bible. I wanted to tell him, "Hey, this is your church, you know! Don't you think you could join us at least for a few minutes?" But only seconds later, he looked up and said, "I think the Lord just spoke to me from the passage He led me to read." And he explained a biblical principle that shaped our discussion for the rest of the meeting.

His input that day wasn't an anomaly. Joe is deeply devoted to God, to prayer, and to the Scriptures. Whenever I talk with him, he tells me what God is teaching him from the Word. A lot of pastors read the Bible primarily to prepare for sermons, but Joe reads it because it draws him closer to our great and loving Father.

And speaking of fathers . . . Joe's childhood was uncommon, having grown up in locker rooms with the most driven athletes while traveling with his father, an NFL coach. Many leadership and family lessons from those travels are found in this book. Joe is passing that legacy down to his children, too, loving and honoring them in their tenacious pursuits of God and His calling in their lives.

A few years ago, I wrote a book called *Leadership Pain*. The theme of the book is that people grow only to the threshold of their pain tolerance. Joe experienced the pain of pastorship and the constant pressure of leading a growing church. Through it all, his pain threshold has continued to rise. In fact, his picture should have been on the cover of my book. Yet, it's not the pain of ministry that Joe would ever dwell on – it's the joy of ministry that he exudes as he inspires and challenges people to confront compromise. Joe has developed an intimate connection with God that has given him the faith to eagerly hear God's directions, instantly obey His voice, and steadfastly follow through to the end. He is a resilient man, husband, father, leader, and friend—one people know they can count on for compassionate support, bold leadership, and plenty of laughs along the way.

The book you hold in your hands encourages you to be aware of potential compromises but stand strong in your faith. I know of no one more qualified to write it than Pastor Joe Champion.

—Sam Chand
Joe Champion's friend

CONTENTS

CHAPTER 1

ALL-IN

January 10, 1987, should've been the worst day of my life; it was the day I was confronted. There are two important days in every person's spiritual life. The day you say "yes" to Jesus and receive the gift of eternal life and the day you become wide awake to God's calling for your life in the here and now. In a small country hospital bathroom, with doctors across the hall trying to save my dad, my hero, my best friend after a cardiac arrest, I said three words to God. "You've got it!" Those became the marking words of *awakeness* to God's purpose for my life.

I wasn't trying to make a deal with God that if he saved my dad's life, I'd fully follow Him. In fact, I'd made short-lived commitments to Christ in the past. This was a "No-matter-what-whether-he-lives-or-dies-I'm-in" kind of commitment!

Just a few hours earlier, while sitting on a deer stand, I'd heard God's voice for the first time in my life. You get the best sleep in those early morning hunts, and as I was dozing off, I heard, "Today will be the greatest day of your life. You'll never be the same after today!" It wasn't audible, but it was so undeniable and out-of-the-blue that I knew it didn't come from me. I wondered if I were about to kill the world's largest deer and start a new reality show called *Deer Dynasty*! I took out an average deer and headed to my uncle's house where I was given the news that my dad was on his way to the hospital after collapsing of a heart attack. This wasn't the "greatest day" I'd envisioned.

On the way to the hospital, I thought about my dad, a successful NFL, CFL, and college football coach who'd picked himself up and not only survived, but thrived after many adversities. As a six-year-old boy, a son of a Mississippi sharecropper, living in a house with holes in the roof, he'd dream of the day he'd escape a life of poverty, and he knew football would be his ticket. He enlisted in the Army during World War II and fought in the Battle of the Bulge. So few of his company

||||||||||||||||||||||||||||||||||||||||||||||||||||||||||||||||||||||||||||||||||||||||||||||||||||||||||

I HAD GIVEN MY ALL IN EVERY REALM ... EXCEPT FOR GOD'S.

||||||||||||||||||||||||||||||||||||||||||||||||||||||||||||||||||||||||||||||||||||||||||||||||||||||||||

survived that they had to merge with another division, the Big Red One. He came home after the war to play football at Mississippi State and in the NFL. Then began his coaching career that moved our family all over the United States and to Canada, where he was head coach of the British Columbia Lions, and where I was born. I was their late-in-life, "Grey Cup" (Canadian Super Bowl) baby.

Jim Champion always modeled an all-in life, whether he was fighting the worldwide threat of Nazi Germany or an opponent in football's biggest stadiums. His three sons followed suit. We all played college football. My two older brothers served distinguishably in the military. Greg ended his military service as a two-star Special Forces Army General, and Keith was a Naval Academy grad, and he retired as a Lt. Colonel Marine fighter pilot. Their lengthy military resumes are light-heartedly followed by mine as a "servant in the Lord's army!" For some reason, before that day in the hospital (where I'd eventually be given the news that my father had passed away) and before my "no-matter-what" commitment, I had given my all in every realm . . . except for God's.

Instead of commitment, all I'd given God was compromise. I'd sat on the fence, wanting to serve God but constantly lured away by my own desires and my own complacency. I was playing football at Louisiana State University, sometimes team captain and always party captain, but the discipline I applied to sports was never applied to my God-purpose.

In *Confronting Compromise*, I'll describe how God brought me to a place where compromise no longer looked attractive. In fact, it became repulsive! The love of Jesus and His purpose for me overwhelmed my previous desires, the things that promised so much and provided so little. Sometimes, it takes a loud wake-up call.

THE REALITY OF COMPROMISE

Few of us think hard about a decision and remark, "I think I'll compromise my values. It's a good idea to compromise my ethics, my reputation, and my legacy. I know it'll turn out well!" It won't. It hasn't. It doesn't.

But it happens, and it happens far more easily than we can imagine. The process is as old as the Garden of Eden and as recent as the last minute. We're faced with a choice—a major one or one of a zillion little ones—and we consider the options. At least one of the options is to take the easy way out, to shade the truth just a little, fudge the numbers a bit, put off something we know we need to do, or tell a "white lie" to get out of a sticky conversation. (There are a lot more examples, but you get the idea.) We take the first step, and the earth doesn't shake under our feet—in other words, we don't get caught—and we conclude it must be okay. So we take the next step, and the next, and the next, until the choice becomes an ingrained habit.

Oh, so you don't think you have a problem with compromising little decisions? Think again. We can identify three main causes that contribute to compromise:

1) Distractions

We're busy. We have the world at our fingertips (or in our pockets), and we feel compelled to be "in the know." We have outsized responsibilities with our kids and our jobs. In the few moments we're not rushing around, we're thinking about the next pressing thing on our to-do lists. In his article, "Diagnosing Hurry Sickness" in *Leadership* magazine, John Ortberg identified two common ways our lives have become far more complicated than only a few decades ago—speeding up and multi-tasking:

> *"Speeding up. You are haunted by the fear that you don't have enough time to do what needs to be done. You try to read faster, lead board meetings more efficiently, write [business plans or emails] on the fly. . . ."*

"Multiple-tasking. You find yourself doing or thinking more than one thing at a time. The car is a favorite place for this. Hurry-sick [leaders] may drive, eat, drink coffee, listen to tapes for [sic] ideas, shave or apply make-up, direct [sic] business on the car phone—all at the same time. Or they may try to watch TV, read Leadership, *eat dinner, and carry on a phone conversation simultaneously."[1]*

OUR PREOCCUPATION WITH BEING CONNECTED CAUSES US TO BE DISCONNECTED FROM WHAT MATTERS MOST.

In what must be the most easily observable phenomenon in our society, many of us suffer from "continuous partial attention." We're always aware of texts, emails, and calls, so we're "always on," seldom if ever fully disconnected from our devices. (I'm looking at you right now!) Ironically, our preoccupation with being connected causes us to be disconnected from what matters most. By being absorbed by the continuous flow of communication, we're continually distracted from people, from thinking deeply, and from God. In this way, compromise isn't just a decision; it's a lifestyle.

2) **Substitutes**

God has made us so that only He can meet the deepest desires of our hearts and give us a transcendent purpose, but many of us—including a lot of people in church—have settled for less. We may go to church

---

1 John Ortberg, "Diagnosing Hurry Sickness," *Leadership*, Fall, 1998.

a couple of Sundays a month, and we may read our Bibles and pray for a few minutes each day, but our hearts are focused on something or someone other than God. Some of us have made our career our highest hope, and our boss, our title, or our salary has become the most important thing in our lives. Some of us have made politics our consuming passion. We eat, drink, and sleep the latest outrage in the news. And others have made their families their highest good. They live for their kids' success. They're "helicopter parents" whose personal fulfillment is completely tied up in their kids' performances.

——

BIBLICAL TOLERANCE IS THE WILLINGNESS TO LOVE THE UNLOVELY, TO CARE FOR THE MARGINALIZED, AND TO REACH OUT TO PEOPLE WHO DISAGREE WITH US.

——

How can you tell how much these (and many other) substitutes have captured your heart? Years ago, William Temple said that our true lord, our real delight, our highest pursuit is what we think about in our "down time," when we have nothing else calling for our attention. (Gulp!) What are your daydreams? Where does your mind go when you have nothing else going on? That's a window on what's most important to you, your real lord.

3) Cultural Erosion

A lot of really insightful books have been written about the effects of modern culture on our grasp of what's really important. We live in a "post truth" world where "my truth" can't be challenged, and those who try to speak for God's truth are considered narrow bigots (and worse!). Tolerance is the highest virtue today, which means people have the right to live any way they want to, and anyone who talks about character and ethics is an enemy. Biblical tolerance is the willingness to love the unlovely, to care for the marginalized, and to reach out to people who disagree with us—but that's not the kind of tolerance being taught in our culture! In this watered down world, people are losing any grasp of the nature of God. Sociologist Christian Smith studied teenagers and their parents, and he concluded that most people today may give lip service to God and the Bible, but they really follow a belief system he calls "moralistic therapeutic deism"—they're convinced they can be good enough for God to accept them, that God really just wants them to be happy, and He's not really that engaged in the world anyway. With this perspective, compromise is guaranteed!

THE CONSEQUENCES OF COMPROMISE

Compromise is so insidious, because we get away with it so often. Sooner or later, however, it catches up to us. I'm not just talking about "the big ones" like adultery, addictions, or forgeries; I'm talking about the full range of excusing lies, rationalizing selfishness, and cutting corners. We could easily identify dozens of consequences, but let me focus on three:

1) We miss God's best.

Jesus pointedly told His disciples (and us) that we have a choice every moment of every day: If we want to save our lives, we need to lose them. If we want to experience real life, we need to deny ourselves (which is saying "no" to our selfish desires), take up our cross (the ultimate symbol of humble obedience), and follow Him. That's God's best, and it requires everything in us because our natural bent is toward selfishness. Our motivation for pursuing His best isn't promotions, control, or power . . . it's love and loyalty. Jesus gave a simple invitation and a profound challenge again and again: "Follow Me." When we follow Him, we're responding to His limitless love and His sovereign power. He is our loving Savior who is also our supremely powerful King. Can we trust the Creator of the universe and the One who sacrificed His life for us to know what's best for us? Yeah, I think we can.

2) We're poor role models.

People are watching. Our spouse, our kids, our friends, our coworkers, and those we lead are watching us like a hawk. They want to know if this Jesus we say we follow is real, and if we're really serious about following Him . . . or not. Lori and I have three sons. They're grown now, but when they were young, we were very aware that they were sponges, soaking up our values, our commitments, and our priorities. They weren't just listening to our words; they had a sixth sense to pick up our nonverbal messages. They could tell if we were serious about our faith in Jesus.

Do you think the people around you are watching you? They sure are.

3) We lack spiritual power.

People who are aware of the temptation to compromise have a leg up. They notice the very real attraction of excusing, minimizing, and rationalizing, so they can fight it. When we stay close to Jesus, we experience the power of the Holy Spirit to give us insight about our choices, patience to trust God when it appears nothing is happening, confidence that God will work in His way and His timing, and monumental answers to prayer. But those who are "lukewarm" are just going through the motions. They wonder, *What's in it for me?* They don't realize the wonder, the beauty, and the power of the Christian life are only experienced when we want Jesus to be honored, not ourselves. And when we want Him more than anything else, He fills us with more joy, love, and strength than we ever dreamed possible.

Let me riff on another familiar trilogy to show the contrast between a life of commitment and a life of compromise. Paul wrote to the Corinthians that walking with God results in our experience of faith, hope, and love. I've found that to be true in spades, but those who compromise don't experience a growing faith. Instead, they're plagued with doubts, "what ifs," and "if onlys." They've trusted in themselves to make life work, and they're deeply discouraged. Instead of a vibrant hope, they're bored because life has little meaning, or they live under a cloud of fear that their world will come crashing down, and they can't stop it. Instead of experiencing the supernatural love of God to care for those who are often reviled or ignored, they're self-absorbed in their resentment and self-pity, acting like victims when they've brought heartache on themselves by their many compromises.

Please don't misunderstand. I'm not saying that if you've compromised, you're doomed to a second-class life. Not at all. The wonder of God's grace is that He is slow to anger and quick to forgive. Jesus has paid for all your sins—little hedges of the truth and obviously destructive choices. You're never beyond the grace of God. But it's time. It's time to do business with God, to turn to Him the first time or the millionth time, and learn to respond to Jesus with love and loyalty.

THREE EXAMPLES

In this book, we'll look at a number of people in the Bible who faced the temptation to compromise, and thankfully, many of them rose to the challenge. I want to highlight three to whet your appetite:

1) Nehemiah

One of the most devastating events in the history of the Jewish people was the destruction of Jerusalem by the Babylonians. The city was ruined, the temple torn down, and many people were marched off to become servants in the city of Babylon. Why did this happen? Because God's people had compromised over and over again for generations. They complained that God wasn't reliable. They worshiped other gods, and they defied God's pleas to repent and return to Him.

Then, 152 years later, Nehemiah made a trip back to Jerusalem, and he was horrified by the condition of the city. The consequences of compromise were evident: the city in ruins, the protective wall torn down, the beautiful gates burned to the ground, and the people living in poverty.

Nehemiah's story isn't just about his incredible management skills to marshal the resources and people to rebuild the wall (in 52 days!); it is about the *meaning* of the wall. Nehemiah's work told the people what was acceptable to God and what wasn't, what was holy and what wasn't, who could be trusted and who couldn't. It wasn't easy. He had to lead his people against internal dissention and external threats, but through it all, he was saying, "Our ancestors compromised, and we've seen the results. No more. Not here. Not us. We're going to be true to God and His ways."

2) Josiah

If anyone had an excuse for becoming a bad dude, it was Josiah. His father and grandfather had been kings of Judah, and they were two of the most wicked and despicable in the sordid history of terrible kings. Josiah came to the throne when he was just a young man, and I can imagine that the people groaned, anticipating him to be like his dad and granddad—but the young guy broke the mold. He raised money to repair the temple, and during construction, the high priest found something that had gone missing years before: a copy of the Bible. I find that to be alarming. God's people had gone off the rails so far for so long that they had forgotten they even had the Word of God! When the high priest read it to the young king, Josiah tore his clothes as a sign of sorrow and repentance.

Josiah called for a time of national renewal, and he had the Scriptures read to all the people. He renewed their covenant with God, and he devoted his heart and soul to the Lord. Then, he launched a reform movement, tearing down the idols, removing spiritual mediums who had taken God's place as sources of direction for the people, and restoring the celebration of Passover. The account of Josiah's reign says, "There was no king like him" (2 Kings 23:25, ESV).

In the history of the church, young people often lead the rest in turning back to God, purifying the church, and having hearts on fire for Jesus. We could use some of that now!

3) Jesus

Jesus was always under pressure to tone down His message and give in to the manipulation of the religious leaders . . . and probably look for disciples who were more perceptive than the ones He had! But He didn't.

After He was baptized, the Holy Spirit led Him into the desert where He fasted and prayed. There, Satan appeared and tempted Him. The first challenge was to make bread out of stones because He was hungry, but Jesus didn't compromise to fill His immediate craving. His feast was the Word of God. The second temptation (recorded in Luke) was the offer to rule all the kingdoms of the world, as if they were Satan's to give.

BECAUSE JESUS DIDN'T COMPROMISE, WE'RE FORGIVEN.

But Jesus refused to bow to anyone other than the Father. Finally, Satan took Jesus to the top of the temple and challenged Him, "If you are the Son of God throw Yourself down from here," (Luke 4:9, NASB) and he quoted a passage promising angelic protection. But again, Jesus didn't bite. This time, Jesus saw that Satan was using the promises of the Bible in a way that tempted Jesus to obey him instead of God.

The supreme temptation in Jesus' life happened three years later in the Garden of Gethsemane when He looked into the pit of hell and saw the immense, overwhelming judgment He was going to suffer in our place. The strain was enormous—His blood vessels broke, and He sweat blood. He prayed in Matthew 26:39 (author's paraphrase), "Father, let this cup [the cup of divine wrath for sin] pass from Me." It was a very reasonable request, but Jesus knew that His mission was to die, so He continued, "Nevertheless, not My will but Yours be done."

Because Jesus didn't compromise, we're forgiven. Because He didn't cave, the door is open to every person to become a child of God. Because He didn't waver, we can call Him Lord, King, Savior, and Friend. I remember the old Andraé Crouch song, "I Don't Know Why Jesus Loved Me." We'd be in big trouble if He had compromised. I'm so glad He was true to the Father, true to His calling, and true to you and me.

DON'T LIVE WITH IT

On December 15, 2020, I woke up, and I could no longer see.

At least, not like before. A cloudiness over my left eye had developed. I knew something wasn't quite right, but I didn't yet realize that something was very wrong. I knew what it was like to have clear vision, and this was not it. My first thought was just to live with it. After all, it didn't hurt. My vision wasn't gone, it was just blurry. However, at the urging of my wife, Lori, I decided to get it checked out. That's when my doctor revealed that I had a torn retina. In fact, he told me that, had we not discovered it, I could have lost my eyesight completely in that eye.

SMALL COMPROMISES CAN LEAD TO BIG CONSEQUENCES

After surgery, things were supposed to get better, but they didn't. A torn retina eventually turned into a detached retina and, multiple surgeries later, I finally find my vision becoming clearer. It's funny how something so small can have such a huge effect. Something I wanted to ignore could have stolen my vision completely. I think that's a reality for life. There are things we live with every day that seem small and insignificant. Not every compromise is a big one. Most are just little compromises that we know aren't quite right, but we are willing to live with them. Small compromises in our faith, thoughts, and habits have a way of throwing life's trajectory completely off. In fact, small compromises can lead to big consequences. Whether you have some major areas of compromise in your life or you're allowing small compromises to slide, I'm urging you not to live with it. Confront it, give it to God, and step up to the calling God has for you.

FOR YOU AND ME, A CRISIS ISN'T A FALLOUT. IT'S A CALLOUT!

MOMENTS OF TRUTH

In my life and in the lives of everyone I know who is walking with God, it appears that God has given us moments of truth when we have to face our temptation to compromise. Sometimes, someone we love calls us to account for our selfishness, and sometimes, we face the consequences of our wayward slide. Quite often, though, God gets our attention when we encounter unforeseen difficulties that are so bad that we can't find any way out on our own.

For you and me, a crisis isn't a fallout. It's a callout! When an enslaved mindset grips people, you are the person who knows that there is something more . . . something greater. Just like the saying "Only the strong survive," there's a group of people who aren't content with allowing a temporary circumstance to take their vision off God. The Bible is full of ordinary individuals who survived persecution, who stood for their faith against the culture of the times. They were undefiled by pandemics or politics and refused to be imprisoned by fear or captivated by social pressures. They were those who stood for their beliefs when beliefs were being deconstructed. They weren't perfect but they faced their shortcomings and would not compromise, and now we can learn from their stories.

THRIVERS DON'T BOW; THEY BUILD. THEY MOVE. THEY EXPAND.

As I've talked to many people over the past year, quite a few have told me, "Pastor Joe, I'm just trying to survive." Surviving is just getting by, settling, or playing not to lose. Coach Dad, who was a defensive specialist in football, would call it "Prevent Defense." He said, "Prevent defense prevents you from winning." In contrast, thriving looks to the future. It doesn't just see an occurrence; it seizes an opportunity. Thrivers don't bow; they build. They move. They expand.

Let me assure you that this book isn't for the person content with a cloudy vision for their lives. Certainly, we need to be honest about the disappointment, challenges, pain, and loss we've endured, but this book points forward—it's about trusting God to turn disappointments, detours, and setbacks into stepping-stones of spiritual growth. It's about remembering what it's like to have a clear vision of who God is and that every action, decision, and response is to glorify Him.

My prayer is that *Confronting Compromise* will help you learn to thrive instead of merely survive, to find and follow God's plan for your life rather than settle for drift and compromise. As you do, you won't be the only one to benefit. You'll have a major impact on your world and make a difference. And hopefully, you'll never again settle for less than God's best.

CHAPTER 2

WIDE AWAKE

You may think I don't notice, but I do. It's actually pretty comical. Some people come to church, they stand and sing the songs, but a few minutes after I begin preaching, I can see their eyelids begin to droop. They've perfected the art of drifting off to sleep while sitting straight up in their seats! If you've ever heard me speak, you know that I can get a little animated at times, but that doesn't seem to bother them. They just snooze away. It's a mystery to me what wakes them up at the end of the service. Did a spouse poke them in the ribs? Did they sense movement around them? Did God set off a silent alarm in their minds? I don't know. But I know they've missed something . . . something important.

If, by some remote chance, you've been in the ranks of the sleepers in church, you're not alone. There's a young man in the Bible named Eutychus. I see myself in him. His name meant "fortunate," and well, my name is "Champion." And like the story of Eutychus, I haven't always reflected my name.

Eutychus shows up in a scene that is at the same time comical, tragic, and glorious. Luke tells us about Paul speaking at a church service in the city of Troas, known as Troy in ancient literature, on the northwestern shores of the Aegean Sea in modern Turkey. Luke puts us in the worship service: "On the first day of the week, when we were gathered together to break bread, Paul began talking to them, intending to leave the next day, and he prolonged his message until midnight. There were many lamps in the upstairs room where we were gathered together" (Acts 20:7-8, NASB). Did you get that? "He prolonged his message until midnight." Paul had a lot to say! My church would likely say the same about me. Luke doesn't tell us the topic for the evening, but in other parts of Acts, we see, that Paul told people that the God who had revealed Himself to Abraham, Isaac, and Jacob, and who had promised to restore the throne of David had actually come . . . and His name is Jesus. And His ability to forgive was validated by His resurrection from the tomb. That's a message Paul never tired of telling.

And he kept on telling it. He probably got great eye contact from the people sitting near him, but one of the people there found somewhere else to sit. A young man named Eutychus found his way up to the third floor and sat on a windowsill. Why was he up there? Maybe the breeze was cooler, or maybe he was like some people who show up at church but sit in the back . . . or in the balcony at some churches . . . or duck out when no one is looking. I always sat in the back of the bus on the way to school, out of the line of sight of the bus driver. I made faces and maybe some inappropriate gestures at the cars behind us! I was in the bus, but my focus was on what was happening outside of the bus. That's how I picture Eutychus. (When I'm behind a school bus today, I try not to look! Those kids can break you down!)

Somewhere around Paul's fourth or fifth hour of preaching, Eutychus sank "into a deep sleep, and as Paul kept on talking, Eutychus was overcome by sleep and fell down from the third floor, and was picked up dead" (v. 9). His drifting resulted in his splattering!

I'd love to have seen Paul's face when this happened. Was he shocked? Maybe . . . maybe not. Luke tells us, "But Paul went down and fell upon him, and after embracing him, he said, 'Do not be troubled, for he is still alive.' When Paul had gone back up and had broken the bread and eaten, he talked with them a long while until daybreak, and then left. They took away the boy alive, and were greatly comforted" (vv. 10-12).

||||||||||||||||||||||||||||||||||||||||||||||||||||||||||||||||||||||||||||||||||||||||||||||||||||||||||||||||||||||||||||

HE ABANDONED THE SEAT OF COMMITMENT AND FOUND THE SEAT OF COMPROMISE

||||||||||||||||||||||||||||||||||||||||||||||||||||||||||||||||||||||||||||||||||||||||||||||||||||||||||||||||||||||||||||

Get that: long talk, dozing young guy, face-plant on the pavement, sudden death . . . no problem. Paul raised Eutychus from the dead, ate a covered-dish supper (and probably served Communion), and kept talking until the sun came up! Imagine the conversations Eutychus had during the night. Remember, his name meant "fortunate." That night, he was fortunate that God had Paul in the right place at the right time to breathe life back into that young man!

Let's go back into the story. Eutychus had the opportunity to hear the greatest preacher the world has ever known (except Jesus, of course), but his heart wasn't riveted on every word. When he went up to the third floor and sat in the window, he abandoned the seat of commitment and found the seat of compromise. Would he have put it that way? Probably not. He would have said something like this: "Oh man, that guy talks too long." "It's hot down there, and I need some air." "I stayed up too late last night, and I'm tired. I'm going where nobody can see me just in case I accidentally doze off."

Notice where Eutychus was: he was in church! Who knew church could be so high-risk?! The point is that it's possible to be physically present, while still being so disengaged from the Word of God, the Spirit of God, and the people of God that we fall asleep and fall away from our purpose. I'm reminded that Jesus instructed us to make this request: "And do not lead us into temptation, but deliver us from evil" (Matthew 6:13, NIV). I take it to mean "lead us not into *too much* temptation, the kind we can't handle, the kind that makes us drift away from God and then fall flat on our faces."

When Lori and I met, we lived an eighty-minute drive apart from each other. It wasn't hard at all to stay awake on my way to see her. Even after a long day of working in the oil field, at that time in my life, the excitement of new love was more caffeinating than a six-pack of energy drinks. But that late-night drive back to my Natchez, Mississippi, home was brutal. It was the same driving time, but I didn't appreciate the destination in the same way, so I didn't have the same energy. You could hear me coming down the highway, radio blasting, windows rolled down, looking a little off as I slapped myself, pinched myself, or sang my heart out just to keep myself awake.

||||||||||||||||||||||||||||||||||||||||||||||||||||||||||||||||||||||||||||||||||||||||||||||||||||||||||||||||

THE WORLD NEEDS TO SEE US LIVING LIFE—ON PURPOSE AND EMPOWERED BY GOD.

||||||||||||||||||||||||||||||||||||||||||||||||||||||||||||||||||||||||||||||||||||||||||||||||||||||||||||||||

It looked strange, but staying awake while driving is really important. So is staying awake while pursuing a life in God. Real Christianity isn't for sleepers! Ephesians 5:14 (NIV) says, "Wake up, sleeper, rise from the dead, and Christ will shine on you."

The world needs to see us living life—on purpose and empowered by God. There are seven areas in this story of Eutychus that warn us to be different than he was—to be wide awake:

1) Opportunity

Eutychus had the opportunity to hear the apostle Paul—one of the most influential leaders the world has ever known, the one God used to interpret the Old Testament and the Gospels for the early church, the one whose zeal for God was blended with genuine humility. Eutychus missed his chance to listen to Paul before midnight, but maybe he paid more attention after he was raised from the dead!

We often think of our careers when we hear the word "opportunity," but it's much, much broader than that. Every person we meet, every moment with someone we love, every challenge we face, and every heartache that tests our faith is an opportunity to tell God, "In this moment, I belong to You, and even if I don't know what's going on, You do. I trust You."

Sometimes, opportunities are disguised, so we have to reveal them. Not long ago, we were on a road trip and pulled into a busy restaurant parking lot. After circling several times, we spotted a car leaving. Great opportunity. Blinkers on, waiting to pull in, and another car whipped in from the highway and stole our spot. That, too, was a great opportunity. Lori decided it was her opportunity to give the driver a piece of advice! But I realized it was an opportunity to show a little wisdom and grace—wisdom for Lori to stay in the car (I reminded her that we were the outsiders in this small-town restaurant we were about to be eating in), and grace for the guy who stole our parking place.

Of course, the greatest opportunity God has given us is to be forgiven by the sacrifice of Christ, to be declared righteous in His sight because Christ's own righteousness has been imputed to our account, and to be adopted as children of God—the highest privilege ever known. In a parable about heaven and hell, Jesus told the story of a poor man named Lazarus (who, by the way, is the only person named in any of Jesus' parables) and a rich man who didn't care at all about Lazarus's condition. When both died, the rich man realized he had missed his opportunity to trust in God and show kindness to Lazarus. Abraham, representing God, told the rich man that it was too late . . . he had missed his chance.

We sense the explosion of gratitude, though, in Paul's prayer for the Colossians: ". . . joyously giving thanks to the Father, who has qualified us to share in the inheritance of the saints in light. For He rescued us from the domain of darkness and transferred us to the kingdom of His beloved Son, in whom we have redemption, the forgiveness of sins" (Colossians 1:11-14, NASB). We were disqualified, without hope, without any way to earn God's love and acceptance, but Jesus paid the price we couldn't pay. He took the punishment we deserved, so we could receive the honor and love He deserves. His obedience became our opportunity.

|||||||||||||||||||||||||||||||||||||||||||||||||||||||||||||||||||||||||||||||||||||||||||||||||||||||||||||||||

THE MORE I READ, THE MORE I CHANGED, AND THE MORE I CHANGED, THE MORE I WANTED TO READ.

|||||||||||||||||||||||||||||||||||||||||||||||||||||||||||||||||||||||||||||||||||||||||||||||||||||||||||||||||

2) God's Word

While he was sitting in the third-floor window, Eutychus didn't appreciate the words spoken by Paul, which were based on the Old Testament and undoubtedly paralleled his letters to the churches.

One of my greatest goals as a pastor is that people fall in love with their Bibles! I wasn't much of a reader growing up and got to college because of my football skills, not my academic abilities. But, after my encounter with Christ in that hospital bathroom, I began to devour the Word like I'd once devoured drinks at dollar-beer night at Fred's Bar during my days at LSU.

In my conversations with people over the years, I've noticed three distinct responses to God's Word: some are *bored* by it, some are *confused* by it, and some see it as *life and breath*. Eutychus was bored with it. I've noticed some people stare blankly when discussing the Scriptures.

Others excuse themselves or change the subject. I get that it can be intimidating at first. As someone who wasn't raised in church, I've been the person in the room who didn't know the Sunday school stories everyone else could quote backwards. But that challenged me to search it out, to become a student, to read this living testament to the One I had centered my life around! The more I read, the more I changed, and the more I changed, the more I wanted to read. I was awakening to the Word of God.

Those who see God's Word as a gift are like Joshua, who heard God tell him:

> *"Only be strong and very courageous; be careful to do according to all the Law which Moses My servant commanded you; do not turn from it to the right or to the left, so that you may achieve success wherever you go. This Book of the Law shall not depart from your mouth, but you shall meditate on it day and night, so that you may be careful to do according to all that is written in it; for then you will make your way prosperous, and then you will achieve success. Have I not commanded you? Be strong and courageous! Do not be terrified nor dismayed, for the LORD your God is with you wherever you go."* —*Joshua 1:7-9 (NASB)*

And they're like the prophet Jeremiah, who found God's Word to be sweet and nourishing. He prayed, "Your words were found and I ate them, And Your words became a joy to me and the delight of my heart; For I have been called by Your name, LORD God of armies (Jeremiah 15:16, NASB).

If I can see God's Word as a gift and devour it so it feeds my soul, you can too.

3) God's House

I've had the privilege of speaking at some of the largest churches in the world. I've also had the equal privilege to speak at struggling church-plants, which is how I'd describe the early days of my church, Celebration Church—sometimes just a couple dozen people meeting in a library conference room. My son Mason, 8 years old at the time, looked at our little library church and said, "This isn't a real church, Dad. I'm going back to Louisiana." He was my sound guy, and I couldn't lose him, so I paid him an allowance to stay! He was too young to realize that the house of God is more than a building . . . much more. When Paul wrote to the Ephesians, he addressed one of the most contentious issues in the early church: Does God consider Gentiles and Jews equal in the church of Jesus Christ? He explained that the cross changed everything:

> But now in Christ Jesus you who previously were far away [the Gentiles] have been brought near by the blood of Christ. For He Himself is our peace, who made both groups into one and broke down the barrier of the dividing wall [that separated the court of the Gentiles from the worshiping Jews in the temple], by abolishing in His flesh the hostility, which is the Law composed of commandments expressed in ordinances [so valued by the Jews], so that in Himself He might make the two one new person, in this way establishing peace; and that He might reconcile them both in one body to God through the cross, by it having put to death the hostility. —Ephesians 2:13-16 (NASB)

I love the boldness of that last part: Gentiles and Jews had been hostile to each other since the time of Abraham, but Christ's death on the cross *killed their hostility* toward each other! In its place, love, forgiveness, and acceptance—found only in Christ—transform individuals, families, races, and communities.

||||||||||||||||||||||||||||||||||||||||||||||||||||||||||||||||||||||||||||||||||||||||||||||||||||||||||||||||||||

GOING ALL IN ON GOD'S CHURCH IS ONE OF THE GREATEST DECISIONS I HAVE EVER MADE.

||||||||||||||||||||||||||||||||||||||||||||||||||||||||||||||||||||||||||||||||||||||||||||||||||||||||||||||||||||

Together, we love one another, support one another, and pray for one another but also work together to build something greater than ourselves. When times are hard, we appreciate the believers we've connected with. In the first years of the church, Peter was warned to stop preaching about Jesus, but he kept it up. Then, he was arrested. His friend James had been arrested, too, and he had been executed. That's the fate Peter expected. There was no compromise in him. Yet, Luke tells us about a plot twist:

> *So Peter was kept in the prison, but prayer for him was being made to God intensely by the church. On the very night when Herod was about to bring him forward, Peter was sleeping between two soldiers, bound with two chains, and guards in front of the door were watching over the prison. And behold, an angel of the Lord suddenly stood near Peter, and a light shone in the cell; and he struck Peter's side and woke him, saying, "Get up quickly." And his chains fell off his hands.* —Acts 12:5-7 (NASB)

An angel led him out of the prison past the guards. When Peter knocked on the door of the house where the people had been praying for his release, they were surprised and thought it was his angel! Peter's freedom came because of the prayers of his church, and he couldn't wait to see his church in person.

Today, church involvement is on the decline. A few decades ago, those who were identified as "regular attenders" went to church at least three times a month, then it dropped to two, and now it's less than two. Are people busier today than before? Maybe, but the real problem is that they don't see God's house—and God's people—as valued gifts. Eutychus's compromise caused him not to connect with the heart of God or the message of Paul, and it cost him . . . but I think he had a very different perspective on worship services after that night!

I can tell you that in the deepest, darkest seasons of my life, when Lori had cancer and when we've faced other soul-crushing trials, God's people have prayed for us, supported us, and loved us through it all. I don't know where we'd be without them.

Going all in on God's church is one of the greatest decisions I have ever made.

4) Godly Relationships

Luke doesn't tell us anyone else climbed up to the third floor with Eutychus. He was alone up there, which isn't ever a good place to be. I know, because I've been there. When I was a little boy, my father teased me that I was good for only two things: cutting grass and tending bar for him. When I was five, I had mastered many of the skills of making drinks. My dad's favorite was Jack Daniels with Diet Coke . . . I guess he was watching his weight. We had a rule in our house: no locked bedroom doors, and no TVs in bedrooms. My dad wanted us to all be together, but just my presence would sometimes remind him of chores he wanted me to do. Back in the day, our TV didn't even have a remote, so I was the channel changer—constantly. Maybe Eutychus just needed a break from the demands of his family. He wanted a little time alone. In our search for peace, we can end up distancing ourselves from those who can prevent our sleep . . . and our falling out of the windows of life to our death.

ON A STRIP OF ATHLETIC TAPE, THAT HE STUCK ON MY DESK, HE WROTE, "JOE CHAMPION CAN STILL BE A CHAMPION." THAT SENTENCE GAVE ME TWO THINGS THAT WERE IN SHORT SUPPLY AT THAT MOMENT: HOPE AND COURAGE.

In the pivotal moments in my life, when I was tempted to doze, trusted friends have gotten into my business to wake me up. They told me what I needed to hear but didn't want to hear. When I was at LSU (Louisiana State University, for those who aren't indoctrinated in SEC football), I was ready to give up for good. I'd failed my physical after another knee injury. I wrestled with the decision. I loved football, but my rehabilitation would take a lot of work and there were no guarantees I'd recover enough to be back on the roster. My best friend Daryl Daye was a graduate assistant coach. He heard that I was thinking about walking away from the team, so he snuck into my dorm room when I wasn't there. On a strip of athletic tape, that he stuck on my desk, he wrote, "Joe Champion can still be a champion." That sentence gave me two things that were in short supply at that moment: hope and courage.

In one of the most amazing scenes in the Bible, Paul and Barnabas were on a missionary journey to cities in what is now central Turkey. When they came into Lystra, Paul healed a crippled man, and the people in the town concluded that he and Barnabas were gods! The priest of Zeus brought flowers and oxen to sacrifice to them, but Paul rushed out into the crowd to stop them. He never missed an opportunity to tell people about Jesus, and he wasn't going to miss this one either. He told them,

> *"Men, why are you doing these things? We are also men, of the same nature as you, preaching the gospel to you, to turn from these useless things to a living God, who MADE THE HEAVEN AND THE EARTH AND THE SEA, AND EVERYTHING THAT IS IN THEM. In past generations He permitted all the nations to go their own ways; yet He did not leave Himself without witness, in that He did good and gave you rains from heaven and fruitful seasons, satisfying your hearts with food and gladness."* —Acts 14:15-17 (NASB)

That was amazing, but the next scene may top it. Jewish leaders, who had opposed Paul and Barnabas in the cities where they'd just visited, came and stirred up the crowd to stone Paul. The people of Lystra had thought he was a god; now they believed he was an enemy! They dragged him out of the city and left him for dead. Luke describes what happened next:

> *But while the disciples stood around him, he got up and entered the city. The next day he left with Barnabas for Derbe. And after they*

> *had preached the gospel to that city and had made a good number*
> *of disciples, they returned to Lystra, to Iconium, and to Antioch,*
> *strengthening the souls of the disciples, encouraging them to continue*
> *in the faith, and saying, "It is through many tribulations that we*
> *must enter the kingdom of God." When they had appointed elders for*
> *them in every church, having prayed with fasting, they entrusted them*
> *to the Lord in whom they had believed." —Acts 14:20-23 (NASB)*

We may think of Paul as a fierce individualist, but he was nothing of the kind. He treasured his dear friends in the faith.

What's your recurring struggle? Is it an addiction? A strained relationship? Unwillingness to forgive someone who hurt you? Deep discouragement over a roadblock you've encountered? Wounds from the past? Hurts in the present? Shame over a colossal failure? Sooner or later, all of us face monsters like these. Who is the person who can be like Paul to Eutychus or Daryl Daye to you? Who is the person in your life who loves you enough to speak the truth, the hard truth, to you when you don't want to hear it? It's that friend, mentor, or coach in your life who can help you rise to the occasions that require untapped grit. Without them, we will never fulfill the fullness of God's desired plan in our lives.

5) Vision

The ability to see is one of the great gifts God has given us. But it's not just the capacity to see with our eyes; God also has given us the ability to see with our hearts through spiritual eyes.

The Holy Spirit illumines our hearts to grasp the truth of God's Word. This vision keeps our focus on Christ, His agenda, and His love for us through thick and thin. It's easy to have a clear vision of the future when things are going well, but what about in times of struggle? When Jesus hung on the cross, where were the people who had shouted,

"Hosanna to the King!" the week before? Where were His disciples? Only John and a few women were with Him as He died. He was executed in the place of a traitor and murderer, in shame, and hated by the religious leaders. At that snapshot in time, Jesus' life looked like a colossal failure, but from God's perspective, it was the most glorious moment in all of history! That tragedy is the ultimate source of hope, love, and life to all who turn to Jesus. In a beautiful statement of this paradox, the fifth century church leader Augustine observed:

> *Man's maker was made man that He, Ruler of the stars, might nurse at His mother's breast; that the Bread might hunger, the Fountain thirst, the Light sleep, the Way be tired on his journey; that the Truth might be accused of false witness, the Teacher be beaten with whips, the Foundation be suspended on wood; that Strength might grow weak; that the Healer might be wounded; that Life might die.* [2]

We often quote a proverb written by King Solomon: "Where there is no vision, the people are unrestrained, but happy is one who keeps the Law" (Proverbs 29:18, NASB).

The word "unrestrained" also means "unglued." When we don't see things the way God sees them, when our agenda is out of alignment with God's, and when our hearts have drifted from God's best, we gradually (or quickly) come unglued. We become fragile, and we fall apart. We frantically try to hold the pieces in place, and we try to look like we're okay, but inside, we know we're coming apart at the seams.

6) Time

What would I give to listen to one of Paul's sermons? What would I give to have a meal with him, so I could ask him a few theological

2 Augustine, *Sermons* 191.1

questions? Eutychus may not have known it, but God had given him a spectacular gift that night. I would think he treasured his time with Paul after he was raised to life and had dinner.

We live at an incredibly hectic pace. We have a lot of "time-saving devices," but they only make it easier to be distracted. Time is a commodity we can never get back. There's only a finite amount of it while we're on this side of eternity, so it's important for us to treasure it. When Paul wrote a letter to the Ephesians (which was also circulated to the other churches), he told them:

> So then, be careful how you walk, not as unwise people but as wise, making the most of your time, because the days are evil. Therefore, do not be foolish, but understand what the will of the Lord is. And do not get drunk with wine, in which there is debauchery, but be filled with the Spirit." —Ephesians 5:15-18 (NASB)

How are you using your time? Do you make excuses for neglecting the things God values, or are you fighting hard to be wise, recognizing that evil is all around us, pursuing God's best, and inviting the Holy Spirit to empower you to be all God wants you to be?

7) Grace

I can imagine some people who, if they'd been in Paul's place when a young man went to sleep and fell to his death in front of them, would shake their heads and say, "Son, you shoulda been listenin'!" But that's not how Paul responded. He embraced the young man and breathed life into him. What a picture of what God has done (or wants to do) in all of us! We drift, we sleep, and we fall in countless ways. The Bible says we were "dead in our trespasses," without hope and without God. Oh, there are people, often in our churches, who have lived rigidly legalistic lives, by the rules, looking down on "those people," and proud to be so righteous!

They remind me of the older brother in Jesus' parable of the two sons. The younger son insulted his father by demanding his inheritance while his dad was still alive, and he blew it all on wine, women, and song (or the equivalent in those days). But "he came to his senses," repented, and came home. His father forgave him and restored him to full sonship in the family. But the older brother, the one who had worked so hard for so many years, was furious that his dad had such compassion for

IIIIIIIIIIIIIIIIIIIIIIIIIIIIIIIIIIIIIIIIIIIIIIIIIIIIIIIIIIIIIIIIIIIIIIIIIIIIIIIIIIIIIIIIIIIIIIIIIIIIIIIIIIIIIIIIIIIIIIIIIIIII

DON'T MAKE THE MISTAKE OF PITTING JUSTICE AND LOVE AGAINST EACH OTHER.

IIIIIIIIIIIIIIIIIIIIIIIIIIIIIIIIIIIIIIIIIIIIIIIIIIIIIIIIIIIIIIIIIIIIIIIIIIIIIIIIIIIIIIIIIIIIIIIIIIIIIIIIIIIIIIIIIIIIIIIIIIIII

that loser. When his father came to the field to invite him to come to the celebration, the older brother refused. The younger son realized his need for grace, and got far more than he expected. The older son trusted in his self-righteousness, and was left bitter, full of self-pity, on the outside of grace, and resenting it.

The point is that we can miss God either way: by running away from God and being bad . . . or by trusting in our good behavior and faithfulness. All of us need God's amazing grace.

Don't make the mistake of pitting justice and love against each other. On the cross, Jesus exhibited both. He died because He saw our lostness and loved us enough to take our place and pay the price we couldn't pay, and His death satisfied the justice of God to punish sin. It's all wrapped up in the cross of Christ. The writer to the Hebrews puts love and justice together as he admonishes us:

> *For this reason we must pay much closer attention to what we have heard, so that we do not drift away from it. For if the word spoken through angels proved unalterable, and every violation and act of disobedience received a just punishment, how will we escape if we neglect so great a salvation? After it was at first spoken through the Lord, it was confirmed to us by those who heard, God also testifying with them, both by signs and wonders, and by various miracles and by gifts of the Holy Spirit according to His own will.* —Hebrews 2:1-4 (NASB)

The writer goes on to explain that Jesus is both our king and our high priest—rolled into one—and He is full of kindness and compassion. He is thrilled when we're honest about our sins . . . because He's already paid the price to forgive them!

> *Therefore, since we have a great high priest who has passed through the heavens, Jesus the Son of God, let's hold firmly to our confession. For we do not have a high priest who cannot sympathize with our weaknesses, but One who has been tempted in all things just as we are, yet without sin. Therefore, let's approach the throne of grace with confidence, so that we may receive mercy and find grace for help at the time of our need.* —Hebrews 4:14-16 (NASB)

MERCY AND GRACE

I don't know what ran through Eutychus's mind as he fell three stories to the pavement that night. Maybe he realized, *This is what I deserve for being so disconnected from God's truth and love!* At some point, all of us need to realize we deserve God's righteous judgment because we fall far, far short of His glory. We aren't pretty good people who need a little help from God. No, we're tragically fallen people who have no hope apart from God's mercy and grace. Mercy means that *we don't get what we deserve*, which is eternal punishment in hell. Grace means that *we get what we don't deserve*, which is a new identity as children of God, His infinite forgiveness, love, and acceptance, and a renewed purpose to live for Him all day every day.

God isn't a cruel, vindictive judge waiting for you to mess up, so He can put the hammer down on you. He's like the father in Jesus' parable of the two sons: longing, loving, and waiting for you to come home to Him. If you've already come to the feast of God's forgiveness and love, enjoy it, and stay by His side! If you're a younger son who has royally messed up your life, your Father is waiting for you with open arms. You just need to say "yes" to Him. And if you're an older son who has been involved in church all your life and tried to do all the right things, but God has shown you that your heart is far from Him, He has come out to invite you in. Take His hand and enjoy His abundant love. People who are all-in appreciate grace because they have probably been afforded much of it over the course of their lives. I most certainly have, and that same grace has caused me to want to do even more for God.

When we follow Jesus, we realize that He leads us into a paradox: The way to new life is to die to our selfishness. The way to power is to be a servant of all. We gain true riches through radical generosity. The way to experience the wonder of grace is to admit that we're sinners. And the source of true strength is to realize we're powerless on our own. The way to stop or prevent drifting is to drop our anchor of faith always and only in the sea of Jesus' love.

|||||||||||||||||||||||||||||||||||||||||||||||||||||||||||||||||||||||||||||||||||||||||||||||||||||||||||||||||

ONLY THOSE WHO ARE AWAKE CAN AWAKEN OTHERS!

|||||||||||||||||||||||||||||||||||||||||||||||||||||||||||||||||||||||||||||||||||||||||||||||||||||||||||||||||

The great teacher and author T. Austin Sparks remarked, "The best way of getting free from our own troubles is to be occupied with the great things of Christ." In today's world, there are so many troubles, things meant to distract us and take away our energy, But there has never been a more important time for the sons and daughters of God to be awake and to be in purpose. Only those who are awake can awaken others!

CHAPTER 3

HARD BUT
NECESSARY CHOICES

E ven though I played football at LSU, as a young kid, I had no desire for the game. My dad didn't care if I joined little league because he had seen so many young people get sick of sports by the time they entered high school or college—when it really mattered. But my mom had other plans. She was going to make sure I played sports, whether I wanted to or not. One day, mid-season, I decided I was done. I wasn't going to go to practice, and so I hid under the bed. I found out that day, you can run, but you can't hide from Mama! I'll never forget feeling her hand grip my leg, as she yanked me right out from under the bed. She taught me a lesson that day that you finish what you start (even if you were involuntarily drafted). There was no compromise with "Mama Sara." There was no quit in her game, and on that day, there was no quit in mine either.

It was several years before I tried my hand at quitting again. This time it was a golf game. I was in eighth grade, playing a junior tournament at Dunwoody Country Club. My score was seventy, and that was just on the first nine holes! It was embarrassing, and irredeemable, so I decided to walk home. By the time I got home, my dad had already received a phone call from the golf pro reporting that I'd left early. My dad said, "That will be the last time you ever quit a tournament!" And it was. I quit quitting that day.

||||||||||||||||||||||||||||||||||||||||||||||||||||||||||||||||||||||||||||||||||||||||||||||||||||||||||||||||||||

IT'S TIME FOR MORE BELIEVERS TO STOP COMPROMISING AND BEGIN CONFRONTING THE WORLD AROUND US WITH GOD'S TRUTH. NOTHING ELSE AND NOTHING LESS.

||||||||||||||||||||||||||||||||||||||||||||||||||||||||||||||||||||||||||||||||||||||||||||||||||||||||||||||||||||

We didn't attend church, pray prayers, or open Bibles in our home, but in many ways, my parents instilled more biblical principles in us than I see in many families of faith. In fact, I once asked them why we didn't attend church on Christmas or Easter, and they said, "We don't mess with God! We don't go to church on those days because we have no plans to attend the following week or the rest of the year, for that matter. You are either all-in or you aren't." In their own way, they were teaching me respect for God. I wish I'd had a Christ-centered upbringing, but what I never experienced was hypocrisy or compromise.

Don't get me wrong—not all compromise is bad. When I want to do one thing and Lori wants to do another, one or both of us need to compromise a bit, or there will be a confrontation, or as we call it, "aggressive fellowship!" In fact, in marriage, compromise is a way to show our love for each other, by giving up "my way" and preferring the one I love. What I'm addressing in *Confronting Compromise* is the willingness, prompted by either intimidation or apathy, to concede moral and spiritual commitments to avoid conflict. If we really care about our friends, families, and the world we live in, it's time for more believers to stop compromising and begin confronting the world around us with God's truth. Nothing else and nothing less.

||||||||||||||||||||||||||||||||||||||||||||||||||||||||||||||||||||||||||||||||||||||||||||||||||||||||||||||||||||||||||

A COMPROMISE IS AN EASY WAY OUT OF A DIFFICULT PROBLEM, AND CONFRONTING COMPROMISE IS NOT FOR THE WEAK

||||||||||||||||||||||||||||||||||||||||||||||||||||||||||||||||||||||||||||||||||||||||||||||||||||||||||||||||||||||||||

AVOIDING COMPROMISE: JOSEPH'S CHOICES

The consequences of compromise can be devastating in the long run. And, avoiding the temptation to fall into compromise is difficult. A compromise is an easy way out of a difficult problem, and confronting compromise is not for the weak. Yet, God reminds us in the Bible that we are indeed able to overcome temptations. Early in the history of God's people, we see several instances of a trust-in-God-no-matter-what mindset that united and sustained them from the beginning. That trust is what helped them overcome temptation and live God-honoring lives.

You may remember the story of Joseph, whose favored position with his father, Jacob, made him the target of his ten older brothers' fierce jealousy. It got so bad they planned to kill him, but at the last minute, they decided to sell him into slavery.

At about seventeen years old, Joseph found himself in Egypt, serving an official named Potiphar. No matter. Did Joseph give up? Did he feel sorry for himself and pout? At some point during that period, he determined to trust God instead of complaining or whining, and God prospered everything Joseph did. Before long, he was running Potiphar's estate. Now the Bible says that Joseph was a good-looking young man, and it wasn't long before Potiphar's wife took notice of him and decided to swipe right and attempt to seduce Joseph. However, Joseph was a man of conviction. He reminded her that he was given authority over all of Potiphar's dealings and had a responsibility to honor her husband. However, in Genesis 39:9 (author's paraphrase), he then says something vital for us to take into account: "How could I do such a wicked thing and sin against God?" It would have been easy for the young man to compromise his beliefs, but he wouldn't because he realized that he wouldn't be simply sinning against a man, but he would be sinning against God.

We need to remember this! When you sin against a man, you are guilty. When you sin against an infinite God, you are infinitely guilty. This is why we need Jesus so much. We have all sinned and fallen short of God's glory. In other words, we have all sinned against an infinite God, and there is no number of good deeds, positive thoughts, or good intentions that can fix that. If we could expunge our own sins, Jesus wouldn't have had to come and die. His death on the cross paid the price for our sins, and when we give Jesus our life, we become one with Him. God no longer looks at us in judgment, because He already judged His Son for our sins. That's the most unfair exchange in all of history, and we are the very fortunate beneficiaries in the deal.

Joseph's conviction reminds me of a story. Years ago, I was on a job with a group of about twenty oil-field workers. They quickly discovered that I was a young, but passionate, believer. One day one of them said, "Joe, we heard that you want to be a pastor, but I believe that you probably look at this kind of material from time to time," and he held out a nude magazine.

I was thrown off guard a little bit, but I replied, "No. There might've been a time in my life when I'd look at those kinds of magazines, but not now."

I could have left it at that, and we'd all have gone on with our work, but I happened to have a Bible in my back pocket and almost without thinking, I pulled it out and said, "This is what I look at now. I care more about what this Bible reveals to me than what those magazines reveal. If you don't know the Lord, then you need to start reading this book."

The guy who was holding the magazine got really defensive, "Don't tell me I don't read my Bible! I am a Christian. In fact, I'm a deacon at my church." Right then and there, he had the audacity to drop the God-card!

People often say that they don't want to go to church because it's full of hypocrites. Nobody likes a hypocrite! In fact, Jesus aggressively— some would say scandalously—pursued relationships with sinners. He went out of His way to show them love and grace. But when it came to religious hypocrites, He had no stomach for them. Literally. It says in

Revelation 3:15-16 (ESV), "'I know your works: you are neither cold nor hot. Would that you were either cold or hot! So, because you are lukewarm, and neither hot nor cold, I will spit you out of my mouth.'"

||||||||||||||||||||||||||||||||||||||||||||||||||||||||||||||||||||||||||||||||||||||||||||||||||||||||||||||||||||||||||||||

YOU WON'T SEE CONVERSION IN OTHERS UNTIL THEY SEE CONVICTION IN YOU.

||||||||||||||||||||||||||||||||||||||||||||||||||||||||||||||||||||||||||||||||||||||||||||||||||||||||||||||||||||||||||||||

He called them out. He even took a whip and turned over tables, because their actions and motives didn't line up with their beliefs and church titles. This deacon in his church is on the oil field mocking me for standing up against him, while he and the other workers were looking at pictures of naked women that weren't their wives. I believe that kind of "Christian" behavior has turned people off to the gospel. You won't see conversion in others until they see conviction in you.

I knew this was a defining moment, and I needed to stand for truth. So I said, "You can't be a deacon! You're standing in front of these guys and instead of being an example of Christ, you're gawking at naked images of women you all aren't married to, claiming to be a godly person, and now you're mad at me? If you've really read the Bible like you said, you wouldn't have that magazine in the first place."

The rest of the group was listening intently . . . very intently! They thought about what I was saying and even began to agree with me, while the man with the magazine started to look more and more uncomfortable. In that moment, he did something unexpected. He began to soften and repent. We actually got to pray together and see God's love at work—right in the middle of that job site!

How often do we compromise when confronted with a culture that has no respect for the things we believe as followers of God? I could have avoided any significant conflict with those men that day, but by speaking up, God's Spirit prompted one man to repentance and led others to respect God's Word. Don't believe the lie that everybody sleeps around, or everybody looks at pornography—that's a lie to keep you bound to such addictions. It's also a lie to believe that if you've lived a promiscuous life or if you've compromised in this area, that God won't forgive it. Maybe you've never been convicted about this kind of behavior until this very moment. That's because the Holy Spirit is speaking to you and showing you that you were made for more than cheap thrills. He's calling you to a higher standard now. You can live for God, and by His Spirit you can resist and overcome destructive habits.

Joseph did that very thing. One particular day, Potiphar's wife made another sexual advance towards Joseph, and he ran out of the room, but not before she grabbed his coat. She used that coat as evidence to accuse him of attempted rape. It's always the right time to do what is right, even if the outcome isn't what we hope it will be.

Joseph was immediately sent to prison without a trial. No matter. God continued to bless Joseph, and soon the warden gave him charge of the prison. While he was there, he interpreted dreams for two inmates, foretelling that one of them would be forgiven and returned to Pharaoh's service. Joseph urged that man to remember him, but upon his release, he forgot about Joseph. With friends like that, who needs enemies?

Joseph sat in jail for two more years. No matter. One day Pharaoh had some troubling dreams that none of his advisers could explain. Only then did the forgiven jailbird working for Pharaoh remember Joseph, and Pharaoh sent for him. Joseph interpreted Pharaoh's dreams, correctly anticipating seven years of abundant harvest that would be followed by seven years of drought . . . and the prospect of famine. Pharaoh was so impressed with Joseph that he made him second in command over all of Egypt. Thanks to Joseph, the nation was prepared for the long drought, and the stored grain provided food not only for the Egyptians, but for Joseph's father and brothers back home. To make a long story short, Joseph's whole family of seventy people was invited to move to Egypt out of gratitude for what Joseph had done.

That may sound like a story with a happy ending. After all, Pharaoh acknowledged Joseph as an amazing leader, and even after Joseph died, his family continued to multiply and flourish. But that story was just the beginning of a bigger one.

AVOIDING COMPROMISE: ISRAEL'S CHOICES

The book of Genesis ends with the death of Joseph, but the first chapter of Exodus fast-forwards four hundred years. Joseph's family of seventy had grown into a massive nation of hundreds of thousands. The current Pharaoh didn't know anything about Joseph. All he saw was a potential threat—and a powerful labor force—so he put all the Hebrews in bondage:

> *The Egyptians used violence to compel the sons of Israel to labor;*
> *and they made their lives better with hard labor in mortar and bricks*
> *and at all kinds of labor in the field, all their labors which they*
> *violently had them perform as slaves. —Exodus 1:13-14 (NASB)*

The new administration in Egypt didn't respect Joseph, Joseph's faith, or Joseph's people. As the people of Israel continued to multiply and became mighty, Egypt responded with opposition, affliction, threats, and hostility. They began to apply great pressure through harsh overseers, hoping to force the people of Israel to just give up and accept the fact that they were slaves. Many were killed as a result of this oppression—even children (according to the verses that follow the above

IIIIIIIIIIIIIIIIIIIIIIIIIIIIIIIIIIIIIIIIIIIIIIIIIIIIIIIIIIIIIIIIIIIIIIIIIIIIIIIIIIIIIIIIIIIIIIIIIIIIIIIIIIIIIIIIIIIIIIIIIIIIIIII

WE CAN ALWAYS CONTROL OUR RESPONSE.

IIIIIIIIIIIIIIIIIIIIIIIIIIIIIIIIIIIIIIIIIIIIIIIIIIIIIIIIIIIIIIIIIIIIIIIIIIIIIIIIIIIIIIIIIIIIIIIIIIIIIIIIIIIIIIIIIIIIIIIIIIIIIIII

passage). Today, God's people still live in a world that resists righteousness and holiness, a world that does anything it can to drive out God's Word from our lives. We can't stand up to that pressure on our own. We require resurrection power that only God can provide. His power assures us that we can withstand whatever the world throws at us—no matter what happens. Instead of compromising, collapsing, failing, or shutting down, we keep growing and thriving. In fact, God's power becomes more real to us during oppression than in prosperity.

We can't control a whole lot that happens in this world, but there is something we can always control and that is: our response. You have a choice. Today's culture will offer you a lot of options. Instead of trusting in God, some people choose to place their trust in positions and prestige, political power, wealth and comfort, favorite sports teams, youth and beauty, and all kinds of other alternatives. I find it interesting, though, how the pandemic put a temporary (but lengthy) hold on our sporting events, social gatherings, and even many of our family connections, while putting a serious dent in our economy. I think 2020 was telling us, "There's nothing you can trust!" We discovered that anything and everything we have been trusting can be taken away in just a matter of seconds. The Bible calls it a vapor. All those things we counted on that were such a part of our lives are suddenly gone, and we wonder what's next.

The Israelites began to pray, worship, and turn back to the Lord. As they did, God began to multiply them. And no matter what was done to the Israelites, they thrived. Just like many churches and Christians thrived during our recent pandemic. If 2020 did anything positive, it disengaged today's believers from the promises of the world and caused us to hunger and thirst again for God's presence. I desire to be purpose-driven, and we are always in our purpose when the presence of God is in our lives.

God indeed heard the prayers of Israel, just like He hears yours, and He raised up a leader named Moses who would lead Israel out of slavery and into their own promised land.

LET'S MAKE A DEAL? LET'S NOT!

God then sent Moses to persuade the stubborn Pharaoh to let the Israelites leave Egypt, but Pharaoh refused several times. Did Moses say, "Well, I gave it a shot" and then accept a life of bondage and defeat? No! He kept going back to Pharaoh to demand release for his people, and God punctuated Moses' requests with a series of plagues. Eventually, Pharaoh began to negotiate. After a plague of darkness where the Egyptians couldn't see one another for three days, Pharaoh summoned Moses and told him in Exodus 10:24 (NASB), "Go, serve the Lord; only let your flocks and your herds be left behind. Even your little ones may go with you."

A reasonable offer, for a change. A decent compromise, but not good enough. Moses told him:

> *"You must also let us have sacrifices and burnt offerings, so that we may sacrifice them to the Lord our God. Therefore, our livestock too shall go with us; not a hoof shall be left behind, for we shall take some of them to serve the Lord our God, and until we get there we will not know what we are to use to worship the Lord." —Exodus 10:25-26 (NASB)*

I love that line: "Not a hoof shall be left behind." Reminds me of that lyric, "I'm gonna ride 'til I can't no more." They weren't going to go until they could take everything that was theirs. Moses wasn't willing to leave anything behind that he might need to worship God after departing. He was going all the way with God—no compromises.

How about you? Are you leaving behind anything that you might need for your journey, or are you committed to going all the way with God? If we want to experience the life that God has called us to live, we must leave nothing behind—not one hoof, not one grain. Pick it up. Get ready to move. Don't leave anything behind. Let's get on with what God has for us!

IGNORE THOSE LIONS

I believe most of us want to do something significant with our lives, building from where we are now. But I hear a lot of people say, "I'm going to wait until (fill in the blank)," or "It makes no sense to build with all this turmoil going on." Let me assure you: building is always part of

God's plan for your life, no matter how bad things are. We must learn to build even in troublesome times—*especially* in troublesome times.

Building and moving are most essential in hard times. When Jesus came to this world in the flesh, it didn't appear to be a good time, but He came anyway.

D. L. Moody, American revivalist, was asked what he would do if he knew the world was ending tomorrow. His reply was, "I would plant a tree!" I've always been intrigued and challenged by that quote. Even if the end is imminent, keep planting life. We live every day sowing into the future.

I've heard it said that when a lazy man looks out into the road, he always sees lions. Rather than get out and do something productive, he says, "I see a lion there. I see a problem. I see unresolved issues." You can't wait until the lions are gone. They're always there, whether real or imagined. For some people, all it takes is to hear rumors of a lion in the road, and they have an excuse for not moving, growing, and building. Scripture warns us that Satan is a roaring lion that goes about seeking someone to devour (1 Peter 5:8), and that lion is always on the prowl.

If you're going to thrive instead of merely surviving, you can't afford to be intimidated by every challenge that comes your way. Surviving is living by natural instinct, focused on self-protection and merely trying to exist, but thriving is living with the support of a supernatural power. And here's the deal: It's a choice. You can decide if you're going to be a survivor and just exist, or a thriver determined to grow, change, build, and make an impact. You get to choose!

You don't have to make a lot of decisions—just one . . . and make it over and over again. It doesn't take great intelligence, training, or advanced degrees to understand this choice. It's so simple that even I can understand it, and I finished number fifty-one out of a high school class of fifty-two students.

Here's the one and only question you need to consider: *Am I going to trust God to do what's best, no matter what?* If you can answer that question affirmatively, and make it an ongoing mindset, you stop cowering, you stop compromising, your life begins to move again, and you begin to build.

This is the mindset you've seen with Joseph and Moses, an attitude you'll continue to see throughout this book as we look at people of faith in the Old and New Testaments. They were determined not to allow anything in the world to disconnect them from what God wanted to accomplish in their lives. You can make that same decision, develop the same mindset, and see God achieve similar results in your own life.

DESTROY SOME FORTRESSES

Your choice of whom or what to trust in can't be a casual decision. You're preparing yourself for battle and deciding which side you will fight for, so it needs to be a committed choice:

> *For though we walk in the flesh, we do not war according to the flesh, for the weapons of our warfare are not of the flesh, but divinely powerful for the destruction of fortresses. We are destroying speculations and every lofty thing raised up against the knowledge of God, and we are taking every thought captive to the obedience of Christ.*
> —2 Corinthians 10:3-5 (ESV)

When Paul wrote this, he was being attacked on every side. Everything he did and every turn he made was met with opposition. He was in a battle he knew he couldn't win with the weapons of the world. So he continually reminded himself that the weapons of a believer's warfare are not carnal, not of the flesh. Victory would require the supernatural power of God.

Paul urges us to destroy speculations and take every thought captive. Maybe your spiritual life is suffering because of attacks by the enemy, or you're being oppressed at work. Perhaps you're mourning the loss of a mom or a dad or another loved one. Or in some other way, all hell seems to be coming against you. What do you do? As you pray, you list each of those thoughts and speculations and destroy them in the presence of God.

You're not alone. We all have those thoughts and scenarios in our minds: *This is hopeless. Nothing will ever be the same. Nobody cares about me! There's no point. Why is this happening to me? Why do I bother to go to church? God, where are You?* We must battle against such deliberations. When we quit living in prayer, when we stop fasting, when we cease to live in the presence of God, guess what? We become vulnerable, open to being destroyed by the enemy. We start seeing lions in the road everywhere we go, and we're paralyzed by fear. We stop thriving, and we begin to settle for surviving, living on our heels, walking in dread, anger, and self-pity when God has called us to be lion-slayers.

Thrivers understand it's the presence of God that destroys those toxic thoughts. Prayer puts us back into the mind of God. It tunes us into His frequency, so we can hear His voice more clearly. Israel did this when they were enslaved by Egypt, and Exodus 2:23-25 tells us how God responded.

1) God heard.

Sometimes we can't even find words to express the depths of our fears and despair. No matter. God hears. In fact, some groanings are too deep for words, but God's Spirit understands and interprets on our behalf.

2) God remembered.

We can be sure that God doesn't forget anything, and He keeps every promise. But prayer helps *us* remember. Have you ever received a gift card and then gone to the store to redeem it? When you get to the cash register, the clerk may ask if you have *activated* the card. God's covenants and promises are always available, but prayer reactivates them in our experience.

IIIIIIIIIIIIIIIIIIIIIIIIIIIIIIIIIIIIIIIIIIIIIIIIIIIIIIIIIIIIIIIIIIIIIIIIIIIIIIIIIIIIIIIIIIIIIIIIIIIIIIIIIIIIIIIII

PRAYER PULLS YOU OUT OF THE STANDS AND PUTS YOU ON GOD'S PLAYING FIELD.

IIIIIIIIIIIIIIIIIIIIIIIIIIIIIIIIIIIIIIIIIIIIIIIIIIIIIIIIIIIIIIIIIIIIIIIIIIIIIIIIIIIIIIIIIIIIIIIIIIIIIIIIIIIIIIIII

Let me ask you: What promises have you forgotten? What gifts have you not activated? We should take a cue from the psalmist. He opens Psalm 103 by saying, "Bless the Lord, my soul, and all that is within me, bless His holy name. Bless the Lord, my soul, and *do not forget any of His benefits*" (vv. 1-2, NASB, author emphasis).

Through prayer, we remember the benefit package of the Lord. His mercies are new every morning, and He remembers what He has promised us.

3) God saw.

Our prayer gets God's attention. It puts a pin on your location and circumstances, and you're able to be identified. Years ago, I was in a stadium with eighty thousand people, and I sensed the Lord whisper to me, "Joe, do you know what will make you stand out in a crowd (or a filled stadium)? It's your prayer life." Prayer pulls you out of the stands and puts you on God's playing field. Prayer puts us on His radar.

|||||||||||||||||||||||||||||||||||||||||||||||||||||||||||||||||||||||||||||||||||||||||||||||||||||||||||||||||||||||||||||||||||||||

YOUR COMMITMENT TO PRAYER DETERMINES THE QUALITY OF YOUR LIFE.

|||||||||||||||||||||||||||||||||||||||||||||||||||||||||||||||||||||||||||||||||||||||||||||||||||||||||||||||||||||||||||||||||||||||

Your commitment to prayer determines the quality of your life. Great prayer, great life. Weak prayer, weak life. More prayer, more life. This is the secret so many people are missing.

4) God noticed.

Finally, Exodus says that God took notice of His people. When believers unite and cry out to the Lord, He definitely hears us, and He responds. That's why we need to pray. That's why we need to fast. That's why we need to be gathering together for worship. When spiritual battles get difficult and the enemy's fortresses seem insurmountable, we need to remind ourselves that God hears. He remembers. He sees. And He notices. Prayer changes things. (We'll pick up the Israelites' story in Chapter 4 and see more specifically *how* God responded to their cries.)

WHEN LIONS ARE IN YOUR PATH

It's hard to think of a better example of someone committed to prayer than Daniel. He was an intelligent and promising young man who was taken to Babylon after the Babylonians destroyed Jerusalem and the temple. He was put in a program with the brightest minds the Babylonians could find, and he consistently excelled under the rule of three Babylonian kings because of his faithfulness to God. When the Persians defeated the Babylonians, King Darius came to power. Perhaps Daniel's rivals saw this as an opportunity to outperform him, but Daniel continued to excel:

> *It pleased Darius to appoint 120 satraps over the kingdom, to be in charge of the whole kingdom, and over them, three commissioners (of whom Daniel was one), so that these satraps would be accountable to them, and that the king would not suffer loss. Then this Daniel began distinguishing himself among the commissioners and satraps because he possessed an extraordinary spirit, and the king intended to appoint him over the entire kingdom. —Daniel 6:1-3 (NASB)*

No matter how hard they tried, the other officials couldn't compete with Daniel because of his "extraordinary spirit." Daniel's long period of loving and trusting God—even while serving foreign kings—distinguished him among all his rivals. It appeared likely that the new king would appoint Daniel over the entire kingdom.

Daniel had an impeccable record. He wasn't late for work. He wasn't skipping out. He wasn't putting personal charges on his royal expense report. No negligence was found in him. His critics couldn't find any evidence of corruption or grounds for any legitimate accusation. They realized his only "fault" was his unwavering devotion to God, and they schemed to find a way to use it against him. So they devised a plan to persuade the king to establish a statute forbidding prayer to any god or person besides King Darius himself.

Daniel knew about this official order, and he knew the consequences for anyone caught praying. So what do you think he did? He continued to pray three times a day, in full view with his windows wide open toward Jerusalem, like he always did. He made no effort to stop his prayer regimen or to try to hide it (see Daniel 6:10).

Daniel's critics thought they had him. They could hardly wait to get back to Darius and tattle. Darius's order was irrevocable, and the punishment was written into the official document. Execution by lions would take care of Daniel for them.

|||||||||||||||||||||||||||||||||||||||||||||||||||||||||||||||||||||||||||||||||||||||||||||||||||||||||||||||||||||||||||||||||||||

TODAY, MANY CHRISTIAN LEADERS ARE OBSESSED WITH BUILDING A BRAND, THE APOSTLE PAUL LAID DOWN HIS BRAND AND PICKED UP SOME BRAND MARKS FOR THE SAKE OF THE GOSPEL.

|||||||||||||||||||||||||||||||||||||||||||||||||||||||||||||||||||||||||||||||||||||||||||||||||||||||||||||||||||||||||||||||||||||

Before we get to the end of this story, let's stop and see what we can learn from Daniel about living in crazy times. How can we place our trust in God and thrive even when faced with critics, problems, and what appears to be a no-win situation? How did Daniel stay strong? We can follow his example in five important ways:

1) Stand for God.

Daniel had developed a well-known reputation of standing for God, which is why his jealous rivals had made praying illegal. Believers are instructed to obey civil laws and governing leaders (Romans 13:1) unless, of course, those laws conflict with the laws of God. When that happens, we need to take a stand for what we believe. We don't need to be arrogant or out of control, but we do need to take a firm and committed stand for the truth of God's Word.

Like Daniel, we must be willing to suffer the consequences for living out our faith. Right now, standing for God can get you cancelled, but the day is approaching where standing for God may get you thrown in prison like Joseph or like Daniel. This was the testimony of most of the New Testament apostles. Today, many Christian leaders are obsessed with building a brand, The apostle Paul laid down his brand and picked up some brand marks for the sake of the gospel. It's time to bring it back to Jesus. Only what we do for Him will last.

2) Worship God.

Paul wrote, "I urge you, brothers and sisters, by the mercies of God, to present your bodies as a living and holy sacrifice, acceptable to God, which is your spiritual service of worship. And do not be conformed to this world, but be transformed by the renewing of your mind, so that you may prove what the will of God is, that which is good and acceptable and perfect" (Romans 12:1-2, NASB).

When we realize we're conforming to the world, we need to work on our worship habits. No matter what, we worship. Daniel knew the lions' den was waiting for him if he continued to worship God, but he was undeterred. Throughout the history of the church, martyrs have faced death when they publicly worshiped God. How about today? I suspect that many of us are unwilling to worship publicly, because we're afraid it might make someone else uncomfortable. Let's take Paul's advice and allow God to renew our minds and transform us into holy, living sacrifices.

3) Serve God.

As Daniel prayed, he faced Jerusalem. Even though he was hundreds of miles away in a foreign country, he remembered his home city filled with God's people. And even as he recalled the destruction of the Jewish temple, he continued to serve God where he was.

||||||||||||||||||||||||||||||||||||||||||||||||||||||||||||||||||||||||||||||||||||||||||||||||||||||||||||||||||||||||||

THE MORE THAT YOU SAY YOU SERVE GOD, THE MORE YOU SHOULD LOVE PEOPLE.

||||||||||||||||||||||||||||||||||||||||||||||||||||||||||||||||||||||||||||||||||||||||||||||||||||||||||||||||||||||||||

Our church was constructed so that we face Austin, as a constant reminder that we're here to serve our city and surrounding communities. We serve God by serving people. The more that you say you serve God, the more you should love people. In fact, if you say you can love God without loving His people, you're either lying or fooling yourself (see 1 John 4:20). By serving other people, we follow the example of Jesus, who said that He "did not come to be served, but to serve" (Matthew 20:28, NIV).

Are you serving God in some capacity? At some point in your life, someone helped you encounter God and start your journey of faith. Now it's your turn to step up to create an atmosphere for other people to encounter God.

4) Pray to God.

Jesus told several parables about prayer. One of the primary reasons was to show that at all times His followers "ought always to pray and not lose heart" (Luke 18:1, ESV). Your prayer life is a prime target for Satan. If he gets your prayer life, he gets your thought life, he gets your faith life, and he gets your love life. If the enemy separates believers from God by diminishing their prayer habits, all areas of life are at risk. If he can keep you from talking to God, he'll start talking to you instead. That's why the Bible says to pray without ceasing (see 1 Thessalonians 5:17). We are to pray at all times and in all seasons, giving thanks to our loving God.

5) Trust God.

Daniel had many opportunities to compromise, but he refused to give in. He stood for God, no matter what. He worshiped God, no matter what. He served God, no matter what. He prayed to God, no matter what. How was he able to do all those things knowing that his enemies were watching him and searching for any reason to bring him up on charges and get rid of him once and for all?

Through it all, Daniel trusted God. Not even Darius, the most powerful ruler at the time, could pardon Daniel. But Daniel wasn't trusting in Darius's deliverance; he was trusting in God's deliverance. And the next morning when he came out without a scratch or tooth mark, he praised God before the king. Anyone who learns to trust God can have a more confident and exciting life—no matter what.

THE RESULTS OF NOT COMPROMISING

It would have been easy for Daniel to put his prayer habits on hold for a few weeks, knowing that people with evil intent were watching him closely. He could have at least retreated to a private prayer closet somewhere in his home. But Daniel knew Whom he was praying to and

Whom he was standing for. His God was worthy of prayer and praise, and Daniel trusted Him to see him through this threatening situation.

Every night when I'd put my three sons to bed, I'd pray that they would love righteousness and hate wickedness. Daniel boldly stood for righteousness, as all believers should. Let us confidently, but not arrogantly say, "I don't participate in certain activities, because I'm living for God." We live in a world in need of more repentance, not more compromise. We need to follow the examples of Moses and Daniel: to stand for God, worship God, pray to God, serve God, and trust God. As we've seen, these commitments in our lives can make significant differences in the lives of people around us.

When we refuse to compromise, and we live with that powerful blend of grace and truth, God will do amazing things in us and through us . . . even in the most secular city in the country. In *The Reason for God*, Pastor Tim Keller reflected on his experience in New York: "I am repeatedly asked, 'How are you reaching thousands of young adults in such a secular place?' The answer is that Christianity has done in New York City what it has done in all the other places that it has grown. It has adapted significantly and positively to the surrounding culture without compromising its main tenets."[3] As you keep reading, we'll look at many more challenges faced by God's people and how He saw them through a great variety of crises. At the end of each chapter, take plenty of time to reflect on that chapter's content. You'll find a few questions to help you consider and apply its principles, and then you'll be able to discern what God is saying to you.

---

3 Tim Keller, *The Reason for God* (New York: Dutton, 2008), p. 42.

CHAPTER 4

PROBLEM-CONSCIOUS OR PURPOSE-CONSCIOUS?

We moved to Austin in August of 2000 to plant Celebration Church. At that time of year, there was a shortage of moving trucks so we mismatched a U-Haul truck with a Ryder trailer on the back, and all of our worldly possessions rolled into our new state. My mom (the one who recruited my unwilling self into sports) drove one of our vehicles and was not as enthusiastic about my church-planting career as she had been about my athletic one. At every stop, she would ask, "What are you doing starting a church? Churches were started hundreds of years ago, and not by a young family of five and certainly not my son!" Then she would offer to turn around and help us go back to Louisiana where we had a stable job at an already existing church. The one who wouldn't allow me to quit little league, was encouraging me to quit before we even started. That was my mom—always the voice of reality, and yet always there to help! In her last years, she moved to Texas and joined our church, and she frequently told us how happy she was that we didn't take her advice early on!

I received even less encouragement from a group of pastors in the city that would occasionally meet for breakfast. At my first introduction to the group, they said to me, "Joe, do you know sixty churches closed last year in Austin?"

I moved here to plant a church, and now everyone's telling me how bad it is to plant a church in Austin? It didn't help when the dotcom bubble burst in 2001. The first year and a half after my move, forty thousand people lost their jobs in Austin. In addition to that, Lori and I were trying to raise a one-year-old, a five-year-old, and a nine-year-old (who was going on nineteen).

The lesson here is to be careful whom you listen to. Sometimes those who are closest to you have the worst advice for you. To be fair, sometimes it's out of a motive to protect you, and other times, they are just negative people. You might remember that Job's wife advised him to "Curse God and die" (see Job 2:9). What a peach! We'll see later in this chapter why that wasn't a great idea.

In my case, I was convinced that God had told me, "Joe, you're on a mission, and you need to listen to Me. Regardless of what someone else says, you'd better do what I told you to do. Follow your calling, no matter what."

Lori and I sat down with our three sons and told them, "Boys, we're in a new home and a new town, and you're going to make some new friends and face some new challenges, but we're making a decision not to just survive, but to thrive." Twenty-plus years later, we still have that commitment to thrive, to trust God, and never compromise on what He leads us to do.

We've already seen Daniel's determination to trust God regardless of the consequences—including an overnight stay in the lions' den. Next we want to look at a man named Job. First, however, I want to provide some background by examining the opening verses of Psalm 24:

> *The earth is the LORD's, and all it contains, The world, and those who live in it. For He has founded it upon the seas And established it upon the rivers. Who may ascend onto the hill of the LORD? And who may stand in His holy place? One who has clean hands and a pure heart, Who has not lifted up his soul to deceit And has not sworn deceitfully. He will receive a blessing from the LORD And righteousness from the God of his salvation. This is the generation of those who seek Him, Who seek Your face—even Jacob.* —*Psalm 24:1-6 (NASB)*

||||||||||||||||||||||||||||||||||||||||||||||||||||||||||||||||||||||||||||||||||||||||||||||||||||||||||||||||||||||||||||

YOUR ABILITY TO THRIVE DEPENDS ON YOUR COMMITMENT TO DOING WHAT'S RIGHT IN GOD'S EYES.

||||||||||||||||||||||||||||||||||||||||||||||||||||||||||||||||||||||||||||||||||||||||||||||||||||||||||||||||||||||||||||

According to the psalmist, what are the requirements for someone who wants to ascend, to get closer to the Lord? He provides a list that includes clean hands, pure heart, honest dealings with others, and a commitment to truth.

We need to understand that God offers a life where we can thrive, but that life must be grounded in the ways of God. Your ability to thrive depends on your commitment to doing what's right in God's eyes.

THE CHOICE IS YOURS

You'll find two kinds of people in today's world—you're one or the other. Some people are *problem-conscious*. Their minds dwell on the problems that they face every day. Whether it's the news, politics, the racial divide, family conflicts and grudges, money, sports, or some other issue, they're always preoccupied with something.

The other group is *purpose-conscious* because they try to be continually aware of and responsive to God's purpose for their lives. But here's the twist: you can shift from one group to the other, sometimes without even realizing it. You need to be quite intentional to move from being *problem-conscious* to becoming *purpose-conscious,* but it's common to see someone unknowingly lose the awareness of God's purpose for their life and drift into a state of problem-consciousness. One day you're right in step with God's will for your life, but then you start texting or posting on social media, and before you know it, you're saying things you didn't even think you were capable of. It's the age-old battle between the flesh and the spirit, always at war within us.

Don't get me wrong. We can disagree with other people. We can express our honest opinions (at the risk of being cancelled, or course). We can even protest the injustices we feel strongly about. But we must do it with clean hands and a pure heart. Otherwise, we soon find ourselves focused more on what's wrong and unfair in the world, rather than what God wants for us. Satan looks for any opportunity to convince you to connect with a power that's not godly, not holy, not true—one that has nothing to do with Christ. In other words, with him.

This was an issue that even Jesus' disciples needed to overcome. They spent all day every day listening to Jesus teach and model the importance of love and compassion. But then, one day when a Samaritan village rejected Jesus, the disciples' first response was, "Lord, do You want us to command fire to come down from heaven and consume them?" (Luke 9:54, NASB) Even in Jesus' presence, His disciples weren't

llllllllllllllllllllllllllllllllllllllllllllllllllllllllllllllllllllllllllllllllllllllllllllllllllllll

PROBLEM-CONSCIOUS PEOPLE ARE FULL OF PANIC.

llllllllllllllllllllllllllllllllllllllllllllllllllllllllllllllllllllllllllllllllllllllllllllllllllllll

always purpose-conscious. They saw a problem, and immediately became consumed by it: "Get 'em, Jesus! Give 'em a dose of thunder and lightning!" But Jesus rebuked them because they were following what they felt rather than following Jesus.

We see from their lives that *problem-conscious people are full of panic*. And they can be extreme in their judgment . . . as in ready to throw fire! When I was a new believer, as an all-in type person, I didn't have much patience for people who also weren't all-in. I could relate to the disciples way more than I could the love and compassion of Christ. In fact, in my prayer time once, I felt the still small voice of God saying, "Joe, you used to be really nice before you got saved!" I'd started to nit-pick the problems in others' lives rather than focusing on Christ, making His presence my peace, and just allowing Him to work in and through me to be an example to those in my life who needed Him.

We need to ask ourselves if we're focused on those problems or on God. The answer determines which kingdom you value most. Problem-conscious people are sour. They're bitter. They're mad because they're so consumed by what's wrong at the moment that they can't see a way out to a better future. But a purpose-conscious person, someone who acknowledges the presence and plan of God no matter what, finds insights that others lack: "Those who have insight will shine brightly like the brightness of the expanse of heaven, and those who lead the many to righteousness, like the stars forever and ever" (Daniel 12:3, NASB).

Purpose-conscious people seek God's ways and ask Him to lead them, guide them, fill them. They not only survive the perpetual chaos of this world, they thrive even in darkness, reflecting God's brightness and righteousness.

Are you preoccupied with what's happening in the world today? Or are you preoccupied with the purpose of God in your life, so focused on the heart of God that you become more concerned about other people than about yourself?

THE PERSISTENT RIGHTEOUSNESS OF JOB

We can all learn something from Job about how to persevere when things aren't going right. His story opens with a description of his outstanding righteousness and the many blessings God had provided. But by the end of the first chapter, he had lost all his oxen, donkeys, sheep, and camels. He had lost all his servants. Worst of all, a windstorm destroyed the house where his children were gathered, and killed them all. (And you think you've got problems?)

As Job tried to work through the pain and confusion, look at his state of mind:

> *"My spirit is broken, my days are extinguished, The grave is ready for me. Mockers are certainly with me, And my eye gazes on their provocation. . . . He has made me a byword of the people, And I am one at whom people spit. My eye has also grown dim because of grief, And all my members are as a shadow. The upright shall be appalled at this, And the innocent shall stir up himself against the godless." —Job 17:1-2, 6-8 (NASB)*

Job was beyond sad. He was low. His spirit was heavy. His future was bleak. His grave was ready. He had already planned his funeral and paid the undertaker. As others had watched his world fall apart, he had become a byword—an object of scorn. Essentially, he was saying, "I am now that man everybody is cursing and mocking. I hear what they're saying about me. My best days are behind me. People are spitting on me. My vision is about gone. My body parts are like a shadow. I have no strength. Good people will look at me and be horrified!"

It sounds like Job has given up on life, doesn't it? But he wasn't finished. Pay close attention to the very next thing he said: "Nevertheless the righteous shall hold to his way, And he who has clean hands shall grow stronger and stronger" (Job 17:9, NASB).

Even though Satan had attacked Job with unimaginable afflictions, even though his world had fallen apart around him, even after his wife had told him to "Curse God and die," even after his friends had barraged him with terrible advice, Job had somehow maintained his purpose-consciousness. He was tenaciously holding on to his no-matter-what commitment to God. Even in the depths of his sufferings, he was living up to the challenge of Psalm 24. Job still had clean hands and a pure heart. He was saying, "God, my whole world is being rocked right now. I'm being falsely judged by others and unjustly attacked. But I know the only way I'm going to stand is to keep Your presence in my life." He had hit rock bottom physically and emotionally, but he refused to compromise.

||||||||||||||||||||||||||||||||||||||||||||||||||||||||||||||||||||||||||||||||||||||||||||||||||||||||||||||||||

REFUSE TO LET GO OF GOD AND KEEP DOING THE RIGHT THING.

||||||||||||||||||||||||||||||||||||||||||||||||||||||||||||||||||||||||||||||||||||||||||||||||||||||||||||||||||

What Job teaches us is that no matter what, no matter how other people attack and ridicule you, you've got to keep your heart right and your conscience clean . . . or you'll grieve God. If you lose the presence of God, nothing good will happen. Job knew that his God was holy and righteous. He's also a God of grace. It's certainly possible to miss the grace of God. Hebrews tells us: "Pursue peace with all people, and the holiness without which no one will see the Lord. See to it that no one comes short of the grace of God; that no root of bitterness springing up causes trouble, and by it many become defiled" (Hebrews 12:14-15, NASB).

Some people treat grace like they've just been given a black American Express card with no limits on spending: "I can do whatever I want now. God's got me covered!" God's grace is abundant, yes, but it's never to be taken for granted. Why do we need this grace so badly? Why is it essential not to "come short" of the grace of God? Because God expects us to be holy *in our relationships with other people*. (Notice, holy, not "holier than thou") Which people? *All* people. That takes a lot of grace.

Our unholiness is at its worst when we're cruel, demanding, or indifferent to people. We tell our staff that the quickest way off our team is to be mean to people. Anytime we mishandle our human relationships, we reflect badly on God. We're bound to mess things up more often than we want, but that's not an excuse to give up. It's why it's so important not to miss any of God's grace as we try to make peace with everyone.

So what do you do when you're being attacked by the devil, or by the world, or by a personal enemy? We all have those powerful internal struggles. What do you do while waiting for God to give you an answer? Refuse to let go of God and keep doing the right thing.

DAVID AND SAUL: A CONTRAST IN LEADERSHIP

King Saul experienced the same struggle. He and his army had cowered in their battlefield tents for forty days as Goliath came out twice a day to taunt them, daring one of them to fight him one-on-one. No one was courageous enough to take him up on his challenge until David was delivering pizzas (bread and cheese) to his brothers in Saul's camp. He noticed that Goliath was mocking the God of Israel, and David couldn't stand by and allow that. He convinced Saul to let him face Goliath, and by the will of God he sank a stone right into the head of the giant. But not as many people are as aware of what happened afterward:

> *Now it happened as they were coming, when David returned from killing the Philistine, that the women came out of all the cities of Israel, singing and dancing, to meet King Saul, with tambourines, with joy and with other musical instruments. The women sang as they played, and said, "Saul has slain his thousands, and David his ten thousands." Then Saul became very angry, for this lyric*

> *displeased him; and he said, "They have given David credit for ten*
> *thousands, but to me they have given credit for only thousands! Now*
> *what more can he have but the kingdom?" And Saul eyed David*
> *with suspicion from that day on.* —*1 Samuel 18:6-9 (NASB)*

YOU HAVE A CHOICE: YOU CAN BE A RAVING MADMAN, OR YOU CAN BE A THRIVING WORSHIPER.

For a short time, Saul was thrilled to be rid of his biggest problem. Goliath was dead, and the Philistines had fled before the reenergized Israelite army. Saul had every reason to thank God and be purpose-conscious. But the very next day he shifted back to his depressive state of problem-consciousness:

> *Now it came to pass on the next day that an evil spirit from God*
> *rushed upon Saul, and he raved in the midst of the house while*
> *David was playing the harp with his hand, as usual; and a spear*
> *was in Saul's hand. Then Saul hurled the spear, for he thought, "I*
> *will pin David to the wall." But David escaped from his presence,*
> *twice. Now Saul was afraid of David, because the Lord was with*
> *him but had left Saul. So Saul removed him from his presence and*
> *appointed him as his commander of a thousand; and he went out and*
> *came in before the people. David was successful in all his ways, for*
> *the Lord was with him.* —*1 Samuel 18:10-14 (NASB)*

Saul had become problem-conscious. Consequently, he became filled with anxiety, and an evil spirit came into him. The only thing that seemed to soothe the anxiety was David's ability to play music on what would be a guitar in the modern day. The moment Saul picked up that spear, he lost his best warrior and his court musician. He thought he was getting rid of a problem, but instead he was creating even worse ones.

After Saul was out of the will of God, it wasn't long before he was out of his mind. He began raving out of control. The word for Saul's "raving" (v. 10) suggests incoherency in the original language. As his problems mounted, he stopped making sense. In contrast, David was very successful in everything he did.

You have a choice: you can be a raving madman, or you can be a thriving worshiper. This country is reaching new levels of madness like never seen before. It takes faithful determination and an ongoing aware-ness of God's presence to rise above the polarization and bitterness so we can experience life as God intended. That willingness is rare. That's why God's people have always been in the minority. It's been that way from the beginning. We know that after Jesus' resurrection, He appeared at least once to a crowd of five hundred believers (1 Corinthians 15:6). He told His followers to go to Jerusalem and await the Holy Spirit (Acts 1:1-5), but when the time came, there were only 120 people there (Acts 1:15). Did the other 380 people really have something better to do than what Jesus told them? Just think what they missed that day.

The problem is that they didn't stay in a state of purpose-conscious-ness. I suspect they ran into some kind of problem, got distracted, and compromised. Satan will always find a way to keep you from going where you're supposed to be. He'll throw obstacles in your path, attempting to turn you around or redirect you. But if you deviate from God's plan and disconnect from God's purpose, what might you miss? Answer: a lot!

A BETTER GRASP OF HOLINESS

Job and David (and others throughout Scripture) demonstrate the marvelous difference it can make to be purpose-conscious rather than problem-conscious. Job faced gut-wrenching losses, but his faithfulness to God got him through the worst, and he emerged stronger and better prepared to face the future. Here are a few foundational truths to help you face your future.

1) God is holy.

The closer we get to God, the better we begin to see and understand holiness. As we examine the life of Christ, we see holiness in action. Peter challenges us:

> *Prepare your minds for action, keep sober in spirit, set your hope completely on the grace to be brought to you at the revelation of Jesus Christ. As obedient children, do not be conformed to the former lusts which were yours in your ignorance, but like the Holy One who called you, be holy yourselves also in all your behavior; because it is written: "You shall be holy, for I am holy." —1 Peter 1:13-16 (NASB)*

Peter is quoting from Leviticus 11:45, so this command to be holy goes all the way back to the law of Moses. Holiness sounds like a churchy term, but if you read closely, you see that holiness is supposed to be demonstrated in everyday behavior—*all* your behavior. It means to be set apart—to stand out and live by godly conviction.

Jesus said, "If you love those who love you, what reward do you have? Even the tax collectors, do they not do the same? And if you greet only your brothers and sisters, what more are you doing than others? Even the Gentiles, do they not do the same? Therefore you shall be perfect, as your heavenly Father is perfect" (Matthew 5:46-48, NASB).

Guess who you're supposed to love? Those that you don't love. Guess who you're supposed to be nice to? Not just the "safe" crowd of your fellow believers. If you greet only your brothers and sisters, that's "canceling" people that you don't like. In our current cancel culture, are you rising above the contentious or apathetic crowd to expand God's kingdom? These extraordinary behaviors are lessons in holiness that take us closer to the perfection Jesus challenges us to strive for.

Jesus' instruction is in the form of a command, not a suggestion, and since it's a command, God expects us to do it. Everything you do and everything you say should reflect Christ.

RIGHTEOUSNESS OFTEN REQUIRES SACRIFICE AND SUFFERING.

2) Righteousness impacts your witness.

Sometimes this word makes you think of "self-righteous," but what it actually means is "right wisdom." Who doesn't want wisdom? We tend to remember Peter as someone who frequently failed to uphold his Lord's standards of righteousness. But Peter eventually learned that Christ's righteousness opens doors for people to share the gospel. When we're living the life that He calls us to live, people notice . . . and they respond. Peter wrote:

> Beloved, I urge you as foreigners and strangers to abstain from fleshly lusts, which wage war against the soul. Keep your behavior excellent among the Gentiles, so that in the thing in which they slander you as

> *evildoers, they may because of your good deeds, as they observe them,*
> *glorify God on the day of visitation. —1 Peter 2:11-12 (NASB)*

Jesus never said, "You shall *do* witnessing." He said, "You shall *be* My witnesses" (Acts 1:8, NASB). Many people don't know that word *witness* suggests being a martyr. That interpretation makes us think of people who have literally lost their lives for speaking up for God, but in fact, in some sense, we all have to die to be a good witness. You have to die to yourself. You have to die to your own agenda. Real discipleship demands death to self so Christ can live in us and through us (Colossians 3:3).

Righteousness often requires sacrifice and suffering. After the apostle Paul's remarkable encounter with Jesus on the road to Damascus, God called Ananias to go lay hands on Paul. Every believer at the time knew Paul's reputation for violent persecution, but the Lord assured Ananias, "Go, for he is a chosen instrument of Mine, to bear My name before the Gentiles and kings and the sons of Israel; for I will show him how much he must suffer for My name's sake" (Acts 9:15-16, NASB).

How do you think people would respond today if our altar calls had this kind of full disclosure? "If you come forward, you're going to suffer. You'll despise many of the demands of living as a Christian. Oh, you will go to heaven and escape an eternity in hell, but it's going to be hell on earth at times. Now, come forward and give your life to Christ." I don't think we'd have as many hands going up. Salvation isn't receiving Christ into our hearts, it's saying, "Jesus, my heart is yours completely!" Then we are to trust the Holy Spirit to be our guide because difficult times will come. Jesus never promised that we, as believers, wouldn't go through hard times. He promised that we wouldn't go through them alone.

3) **Obedience affects your future.**

Remember what Job realized in the depths of his sufferings: "The righteous will hold to his way, and the one who has clean hands will grow stronger and stronger" (Job 17:9, NASB). When you love what's right, you love what God loves. The righteous will obey the ways of God, and their future will reveal God's faithfulness in ways they couldn't even imagine.

Let me be clear: When I say obey the ways of God, I'm not just saying, "Be good." The world says to be good, and even to be spiritual, but that's a far cry from being godly. You can't be truly good without God, and you can't be truly spiritual without the Holy Spirit. "Good" doesn't equate to "godly." Do you see the difference?

Peter expands on Job's insights on suffering. He writes: "For this finds favor, if for the sake of conscience toward God a person endures grief when suffering unjustly. For what credit is there if, when you sin and are harshly treated, you endure it with patience? But if when you do what is right and suffer for it you patiently endure it, this finds favor with God" (1 Peter 2:19-20, NASB).

Your obedience to God's ways, refined through patience during suffering, puts the favor of God on your future.

Peter continues:

> *For you have been called for this purpose, because Christ also suffered for you, leaving you an example, so that you would follow in His steps, He who committed no sin, nor was any deceit found in His mouth; and while being abusively insulted, He did not insult in return; while suffering, He did not threaten, but kept*

entrusting Himself to Him who judges righteously. —*1 Peter 2:21-23 (NASB)*

My parents were very loving, but they expected one hundred percent obedience, Also, they believed that the teacher, the coach or whatever authority was always right. This became a problem when I didn't do my homework . . . repeatedly. After several warnings, Mrs. Smith said four words that shook me, "I'm calling your parents!" For the next several nights, I took the phone (with an extra-long cord) down into the basement, and each night, answered the phone and gave excuses as to where my parents were. I was spinning a web of lies! But there was a day of reckoning, the day I wasn't home to answer the phone. We've all been there. We've all hidden disobedience, and then been found out.

We're going to stand before a loving God one day, at the end of our lives. No more able will we be able to hide the phone. He will then be our judge. How we respond to Him now determines what happens on that day. Again, I reiterate that "all have sinned and fall short of the glory of God" (Romans 3:23, NIV), but that knowledge should be a motivation to turn to God for forgiveness and restoration, not an excuse to keep on sinning. God calls people to change, to obey His commands, to be different from the world, and Peter says your future depends on it. Your business depends on it. Your kids depend on it. The future of this country depends upon holy and righteous people.

4) It is your responsibility.

How can you become more like Christ? Well, I'm going to show you what the Bible says: "Therefore, having these promises, beloved, let's cleanse ourselves from all defilement of flesh and spirit, perfecting holiness in the fear of God" (2 Corinthians 7:1, NASB). Did you see that? Does it say, "You cleanse me, God"? No, it says, "Let's cleanse ourselves."

IIIIIIIIIIIIIIIIIIIIIIIIIIIIIIIIIIIIIIIIIIIIIIIIIIIIIIIIIIIIIIIIIIIIIIIIIIIIIIIIIIIIIIIIIIIIIIIIIIIIIIIIIIIIIIIIIIIIIIIIIIIIII

THE HOLY SPIRIT BRINGS YOU TO THE WATER BUT IT'S UP TO YOU TO DRINK.

IIIIIIIIIIIIIIIIIIIIIIIIIIIIIIIIIIIIIIIIIIIIIIIIIIIIIIIIIIIIIIIIIIIIIIIIIIIIIIIIIIIIIIIIIIIIIIIIIIIIIIIIIIIIIIIIIIIIIIIIIIIIII

Let's get things straight. God justifies us when we put our faith in Christ. It is faith alone that makes us righteous, meaning that when we stand before God one day, He sees Christ's righteousness instead of our sin.

But faith doesn't sanctify you. It doesn't cleanse you. That's your job. The Holy Spirit brings you to the water, but it's up to you to drink. A lot of people come to me and say something like, "I'm praying for this spirit of lying to come out of my life." I tell them, "No, it's not a spirit of lying. You're just a liar. Stop lying. Stop blaming God, when God says you have a responsibility. The Holy Spirit gives you the power to change, so change."

After Jesus forgave the woman who had been caught in adultery, what did He tell her? "I know you're not responsible for your actions"? No. He said, "From now on stop sinning" (see John 8:11). Now, this woman had just met Him. He's talking to a woman who is as green as she can be when it comes to the things of God, yet He's already given her a call to "right wisdom." He's telling her compassionately but firmly, "You got yourself into this. But now that you're out, don't put yourself back into it."

||||||||||||||||||||||||||||||||||||||||||||||||||||||||||||||||||||||||||||||||||||||||||||||||||||||

THE SPIRIT OF GOD WILL GIVE YOU ASSURANCE, DIRECTION, PEACE, AND COURAGE.

||||||||||||||||||||||||||||||||||||||||||||||||||||||||||||||||||||||||||||||||||||||||||||||||||||||

THE WORK OF THE SPIRIT

The Spirit of God is always available to us. The power of God is mightier than any problem we can face. So why are so many of us problem-conscious rather than purpose-conscious?

Take hope from the story of Job. He experienced more pain and suffering than most of us ever will, and he never did get the answers he was searching for (That's a revelation right there!), yet he never lost his sense of God's presence. He was determined to be faithful, no matter what, and he persevered. His future became even more blessed than before (Job 42:12).

See for yourself. The next time a difficult problem begins to divert your attention from the Lord, make the intentional choice to remain purpose-conscious. Tell yourself, "My life is going to be better because of today." And then wait in eager anticipation for what God is about to show you. The Spirit of God will give you assurance, direction, peace, and courage. Count on it.

CHAPTER 5

KEEP MOVING FORWARD

I remember the first San Antonio Spurs game Lori and I ever went to. We were extremely budget conscious at the time (okay, BROKE!), but we scraped together for a much-needed night out. Along the way, we stopped and ate some cheap barbeque (which I regret to this day), and then bought $17 tickets to the game. Of course, we were in the nosebleed section, barely able to see the tiny players on the court far below.

It was the glory days of the San Antonio Spurs, and before long, they were running away with the game. By late in the third quarter, we could see many of the seats below us emptying out, so we made our move to seats near the court. For most of the fourth quarter, we saw a more engaging—and life-sized—game. All the while hoping that no one would come ask to see our tickets. It was risky to move from the cheap seats to the floor level, but we weren't about to let those seats go to waste, and we weren't content with settling in the nosebleed section when we had a better opportunity.

In the same manner, I've always prayed, "God, I want to reach the city of Austin for You. I want whatever piece of the pie You have for me, and if there are other unclaimed pieces of pie out there, meant for other people, I'll take those too!" If you ever go out to dinner with me, you'll know that nothing good will go to waste. I'll eat off your plate, even if we've just met!

IF YOU AREN'T WHERE YOU WANT TO BE, KEEP MOVING FORWARD.

Maybe you can identify (besides the eating off of others' plates part). Maybe you, too, are a person who doesn't let an opportunity or some good, available seats go to waste. God wired you that way, and it's time to focus that towards the kingdom of God. I'm thinking about that game as I'm writing this chapter, because I want to share what I experienced that night: *If you aren't where you want to be, keep moving forward.* Let's look at a couple of biblical accounts that make that point even stronger.

THE ISRAELITES AT THE RED SEA

You may know this story if you've spent any time in Sunday school or children's church. But I want to highlight some points of great significance that many of us seem to miss.

In Chapter 3 we saw that the Israelites had finally been allowed to leave their bondage in Egypt. As it turned out, they weren't gone long before Pharaoh changed his mind and led the entire Egyptian army after them. God's people were camped beside the Red Sea, and seemingly had nowhere to go as the Egyptian chariots came bearing down on them from behind:

> *As Pharaoh approached, the sons of Israel looked, and behold, the Egyptians were coming after them, and they became very frightened; so the sons of Israel cried out to the LORD. Then they said to Moses, "Is it because there were no graves in Egypt that you have taken us away to die in the wilderness? Why have you dealt with us in this way, bringing us out of Egypt? Is this not the word that we spoke to you in Egypt, saying, 'Leave us alone so that we may serve the Egyptians'? For it would have been better for us to serve the Egyptians than to die in the wilderness!"* —Exodus 14:10-12 (NASB)

Pharaoh had begun to think it was a big mistake to let all that manpower—all those human resources—just walk away. Who was going to build his cities and monuments now? He determined to bring them back. Seeing the approaching army made the Israelites shake in their sandals, and suddenly, slavery in Egypt didn't look so bad after all! They hadn't been gone long, but they were already revising their history. They blamed Moses for bringing them out into the wilderness, although *they* had been the ones crying out to God to leave Egypt (Exodus 2:23-25). *They* were the ones who were fed up with the harshness of the Egyptian taskmasters, yet they were ready to go back to that miserable lifestyle.

What was Moses to do? Pharaoh wanted those people back, and now they were ready to comply. Human nature hasn't changed much since then, this is the way it'll always be in your journey. You'll start to make progress but will then run into a problem or an obstacle and wonder, *Did I make the right decision? Did I go in the right direction?*

Moses ignored their complaints and addressed their desperation:

> *But Moses said to the people, "Do not fear! Stand by and see the salvation of the LORD, which He will perform for you today; for the Egyptians whom you have seen today, you will never see them again, ever. The LORD will fight for you, while you keep silent." Then the LORD said to Moses, "Why are you crying out to Me? Tell the sons of Israel to go forward." —Exodus 14:13-15 (NASB)*

PRAYER SHOULD INSPIRE ACTION TO ENGAGE IN THE OPPORTUNITY WHERE GOD IS LEADING US.

Be sure to notice God's response. First, He asks, "Why are you crying out to Me?" I sense a little bit of frustration in God's voice there. I can surmise that Moses had heard from God already and probably was dragging his feet even though he knew what he needed to do. This wasn't a time to keep praying. It was a time to take action!

Be honest. Have you ever used prayer as a delaying tactic, because you were reluctant to do what you felt God leading you to do? Instead of acting, we pray some more. We intercede for others. We fast. We wait upon the Lord . . . and wait . . . and wait. Most of the time, that's perfectly good and right, but here God tells Moses that it's time to stop praying. Yes, I know we are told to "pray without ceasing" (1

Thessalonians 5:17, ESV), but that command requires that we act *while* we pray, or we would never get anything done! Prayer should inspire action to engage in the opportunity where God is leading us. We should never use prayer as a cover for our reluctance.

And then notice what God says next: "Go forward." With all the military might of Egypt descending on them, that was certainly sound advice. The only problem was that they were at the beach, staring into the vast waters of the Red Sea! Going forward looked like a very wet suicide! That's why this wasn't the time to pray. This wasn't the time to cry out. It was time to *move*, to go forward.

||||||||||||||||||||||||||||||||||||||||||||||||||||||||||||||||||||||||||||||||||||||||||||||||||||||||||||||||||||

IF GOD TELLS YOU TO DO SOMETHING, HE'LL ALSO PROVIDE A WAY FOR YOU TO DO IT.

||||||||||||||||||||||||||||||||||||||||||||||||||||||||||||||||||||||||||||||||||||||||||||||||||||||||||||||||||||

In this case, God told Moses to raise his staff over the sea. When he did, the waters parted, God ran interference with the Egyptians while the Israelites moved safely to the other side, and the Egyptians all drowned when they tried to follow God's people (Exodus 14:16-31). Here, Moses and the Israelites learned that *if God tells you to do something, He'll also provide a way for you to do it*. Moses' staff was a symbol of God's authority, and with it, Moses could go wherever God directed him, even across a sea on dry land between walls of water. Two thirds of God's name is "GO" so when He tells you to do so, don't back up. Don't back down. Don't quit.

A LIFE ON THE MOVE

But how does Moses' story apply to God's people today? God's lessons for Israel are directly applicable to the church which you are a part of if you are a believer. In fact, the New Testament refers to the Israelites as "the assembly in the wilderness" (Acts 7:38, NIV), and the word for "assembly" is *ecclesia*, often translated as "church." A church may have buildings, but the church isn't a building; it's a people. A people that God is calling to move forward even when it seems like there's no path before us. We pray for God to make a way; He tells us to trust Him and walk.

Real Christianity is a 24/7 commitment of total obedience to God, not just a weekend service. We can become quite unsettled when we sense God saying, "It's time to quit playing. It's time to stop stalling and start moving forward—directly through that huge problem you see in front of you."

I recently had one of the most uplifting conversations I've had in a long while. I pulled into the church parking lot one Sunday morning and rolled down the car window to speak to one of our attendants. We exchanged the usual "How're you doing?" And then I asked, "How's your work?"

He replied, "Pastor Joe, I'm actually not working right now. For the first time in my life, at 58, I'm without a job, but I believe this is God working in my life. To be honest, I've had the god of money for most of my life, until this year. Now I have to depend on the Lord. I can see I've been living a pseudo-Christian life . . . a double life. But now, for the first time, I have a real Christian life where God is going to have to provide." Cars were backing up behind me as he opened up, but we were having a God moment, and no one seemed to mind.

His words have stayed with me, especially what he said about leading a double life. He was making the same observation as James did in the New Testament:

> *If any of you lacks wisdom, let him ask of God, who gives to all generously and without reproach, and it will be given to him. But he must ask in faith without any doubting, for the one who doubts is like the surf of the sea, driven and tossed by the wind. For that person ought not to expect that he will receive anything from the Lord, being a double-minded man, unstable in all his ways.* —James 1:5-8 (NASB)

Let me ask you, do you tend to split your week between "God's time" and "my time"? Lots of people seem to think that Sunday church hours, ministry hours throughout the week, prayer times, and such are "God's time," and all the other hours are for the necessities of life: work, chores, sleep, sports, or whatever—and have very little to do with God. That's a double-minded outlook, and James warns us that this mindset makes us unstable. In reality, God's time is seven days a week, twenty-four hours a day. You're no more holy on Sundays than you are at a business meeting at work, while cooking breakfast for the kids, watching Monday Night Football, or doing anything else.

The problem boils down to a lack of spiritual capacity, an incomplete spiritual understanding. When you're lacking spiritual capacity, you're more emotional and intellectual than spiritual. Then, when faced with threats, attacks, complaints, and confusion, you respond with fear rather than faith. Instead of standing strong, carrying on, and then moving forward, you become offended, critical, or frightened. You stop moving.

Even the best of us can become double-minded at times. Jesus once said that the greatest man born among women was John the Baptist (Matthew 11:11). John had baptized Jesus. He witnessed the Spirit of God descend on Jesus. He heard the voice of the Father say, "This is My beloved Son, with whom I am well pleased" (see Matthew 3:13-17). But later, John had been arrested by Herod and thrown into prison. While in jail, he heard about Jesus doing great works for other people, which seemed to confuse him. John sent some of his disciples to Jesus ask, "Are You the Coming One, or are we to look for someone else?" (Matthew 11:3, NASB)

SOMETIMES THE ANSWER ISN'T HARD TO FIND, SOMETIMES IT'S JUST HARD TO ACCEPT.

Jesus told John's disciples to tell John that blind people were seeing again, lame people were walking again, deaf people were hearing again, dead people were being raised back to life, and poor people were hearing the good news of God's kingdom (Matthew 11:4-5). And then Jesus added a peculiar statement: "And blessed is any person who does not take offense at Me" (Matthew 11:6, NASB).

The word for "offense" in this passage comes from the Greek word *skandalizo* which means "to be entrapped, to trip up, to offend, to entice to sin." Jesus is saying, "Blessed is He who will not find me to be a stumbling block or will not stumble at me." We are all going to have opportunities to be offended with Christ.

I've heard a lot of people say, "Pastor, I'm so mad at God!" I tell them, "God can handle your anger. Still, don't allow an offense to come between you and God, because when you find yourself sick, without a job, flat on your back, or in some other kind of a wilderness, you may go to the wrong places emotionally and spiritually for answers, when God has already given you the answer. That is to trust God no matter what. Sometimes the answer isn't hard to find, sometimes it's just hard to accept. Your blessing will be in *not being offended* at God. Your circumstances can help you develop a no-matter-what faith."

‖‖

THE DAY YOU STOP GROWING, YOU STOP LIVING AS GOD DESIRES.

‖‖

Here's another piece of valuable insight from this account of Jesus and John the Baptist. After Jesus sends away John's disciples, He *then* turns to the crowds of people around Him and begins to lavish praise on John (Matthew 11:7-15). Why didn't He say that before John's disciples left?

God sometimes doesn't say what we want to hear. We don't hear an "atta boy" after every good deed: "You went to church today. You're so amazing!", or "You helped jump-start your neighbor's car battery. Awesome!" No. That's not how it works.

John the Baptist was as committed as anyone could be, but there is always room for improvement in our spiritual development. The day you stop growing, you stop living as God desires. Jesus told people,

"Follow Me," but I think we try to reverse those roles. We get things backwards. We expect Him to be on call all the time whenever we need something.

Years ago, five pastor friends and I took our families to Disney World for a special promotion. We split the cost and paid for a tour that took us through all the rides and attractions by taking a van that went through back doors and shortcuts unavailable to all the folks waiting in line. During one of our van rides, I asked our hostess about the most unique experience she'd ever had on these tours. She told me about a Middle Eastern royal group of about fifty people: the king, his family, and an entourage of attendants. She said that regardless of height no one in the group could appear taller than the king, even if it required bending over and crouching as they walked.

But the most interesting thing, she said, was that one person in the entourage was there because he was a perfect organ match for the king. If anything at all happened to the king, that person could provide a blood transfusion or organ donation. (What if the king needed a heart? Don't you imagine that guy squirmed every time the king ate a hot dog or funnel cake?)

I think that's the backwards outlook we sometimes develop in our relationship with Jesus. We read that He "did not come to be served, but to serve" (Matthew 20:28, NIV). Do we then envision Jesus walking around behind us, stooping so He doesn't appear taller, ready to jump into action anytime we might need something? If so, we need to read the rest of that verse and rethink that perception. Jesus' primary act of service was "to give His life as a ransom for many." He modeled service to demonstrate how *we're* supposed to live and relate to others.

We should respond by being thankful servants of our Lord and Master. Let's never presume it's His job to spare us from every possible discomfort. These are places in our faith where we need to grow. There are blessings that God has for those walking in His ways, but there are also challenges we will face along the journey. Thankfully, He will take the journey with us.

MOVING FORWARD NO MATTER

What does a forward-moving life look like? Let's examine a few characteristics.

1) A forward-moving life will see miracles.

Most believers agree that everything about God is miraculous, beyond human understanding and description. Beyond that, however, some say that miracles aren't that important. Oh, yes, they are! Our faith is grounded in miracles. What is more miraculous than a virgin birth or a Savior rising from the dead and then ascending into heaven?

Some are cautious because Jesus rebuked those who kept demanding to see Him perform miracles, calling them "an evil and adulterous generation" (Matthew 12:39, ESV; see also Luke 11:29). But those people were insisting on miracles as proof of Jesus' power before making any kind of commitment to Him. We can confidently pray for miracles, because we've already experienced His salvation—the greatest miracle of all—and we know the power He can provide.

Scripture tells us that "the god of this world has blinded the minds of the unbelieving so that they will not see the light of the gospel of the glory of Christ, who is the image of God" (2 Corinthians 4:4, NASB). Satan may be the god of this world, but the one true God frequently disrupts that world by asserting His authority with the miraculous.

Miracles didn't stop with Jesus. He is the same yesterday, today, and forever. The same Holy Spirit is here, and God wants us to see His miraculous power like never before. I believe we're going to see it in the days ahead. For a while now, we've been taking comfort in a nation and a world that we've really loved, but recently all of that has been disrupted. I really do believe miraculous things are going to come from it all as people begin to seek God more intentionally than ever before.

2) A forward-moving life will have opposition.

We can no longer plan for *if* we have opposition; it's *when*. Jesus said, "If the world hates you, you know that it has hated me before it hated you. If you were of the world, the world would love you as its own; but because you are not of the world, but I chose you out of the world, because of this the world hates you" (John 15:18-19, ESV). You've changed loyalties, and nobody likes people who leave them.

When I got saved at LSU, I was playing football. I went from being the team party captain to the team chaplain, literally overnight. When my buddies saw my transformation, they immediately accused me: "You're leaving us. Why are you doing this to us?"

Eventually they saw that my decision didn't exclude them . . . it included Jesus. But God did a purging in my life—I knew I had to get out of my sinful habits and involvements. I also just needed to remove some simple distractions that weren't necessarily sinful at all. As I did, I began to sense opposition from people. Of course, I didn't start condemning them or preaching about their evil choices. I simply communicated that I had made Jesus my Lord and Savior, and they realized that He was not their Lord, not their Savior. Not yet. They could see I wasn't the same guy anymore, which raised questions in their minds:

What about me? How does God see me? Jesus told His followers to expect this kind of reaction:

> *"Remember the word that I said to you, 'A slave is not greater than his master.' If they persecuted Me, they will persecute you as well; if they followed My word, they will follow yours also. But all these things they will do to you on account of My name because they do not know the One who sent Me. If I had not come and spoken to them, they would not have sin; but now they have no excuse for their sin."*—*John 15:20-22 (NASB)*

Some people simply don't want Christ. They don't want Christians. They don't want anyone to invade their space. They don't want to be accountable in their morality. But they realize that there's more to life than the hustle. Believers, simply by reflecting the light of God in their lives, remind them of the truth they stubbornly keep resisting.

3) A forward-moving life will not be ashamed of the name of Jesus.

There's a moment in the life of Peter where he and John were on trial, and he makes one of the most profound statements in the Bible:

> *By the name of Jesus Christ the Nazarene, whom you crucified, whom God raised from the dead—by this name this man stands here before you in good health. He is the stone which was rejected by you, the builders, but which became the chief cornerstone. And there is salvation in no one else; for there is no other name under heaven that has been given among mankind by which we must be saved.* —*Acts 4:10-12 (NASB)*

Without Jesus, there's no other way to the Father, no other door to the kingdom of God. This is probably the most irritating statement that the world can hear—that they don't have a choice in the matter. No one else can save them. They can't save themselves, and they can't be saved by their goodness or any other "good works." Jesus is Lord and Savior because He's God. The Father bestowed on Jesus "the name that is above every name" (Philippians 2:9, NIV). After His resurrection, Jesus prompted His disciples to proclaim repentance for the forgiveness of sins to all nations in His name (Luke 24:47). It's the name His disciples continue to proclaim to this day.

IIIIIIIIIIIIIIIIIIIIIIIIIIIIIIIIIIIIIIIIIIIIIIIIIIIIIIIIIIIIIIIIIIIIIIIIIIIIIIIIIIIIIIIIIIIIIIIIIIIIIIIIIIIIIIIIIIIIIIIIIIIIIIIIIIIIII

WHENEVER THE BODY OF CHRIST SOFTENS ITS COMMITMENT TO GOD AND BEGINS TO INTEGRATE HUMANISTIC CONCEPTS, IT'S NO LONGER A CHURCH.

IIIIIIIIIIIIIIIIIIIIIIIIIIIIIIIIIIIIIIIIIIIIIIIIIIIIIIIIIIIIIIIIIIIIIIIIIIIIIIIIIIIIIIIIIIIIIIIIIIIIIIIIIIIIIIIIIIIIIIIIIIIIIIIIIIIIII

4) A forward-moving life will obey God more than man.

Jesus had already tried to prepare His disciples for the times when their loyalty to Christ would be tested. One day He talked about a world of chaos and conflict, as He was preparing to send them out into it "as sheep in the midst of wolves" (Matthew 10:16, ESV). He cautioned them, "Do not be afraid of those who kill the body but are unable to kill the soul; but rather fear Him who is able to destroy both soul and body in hell" (Matthew 10:28, NASB).

A healthy fear of the Lord is the beginning of wisdom (Psalm 111:10). Wisdom starts with having such a deep reverence for God that we're scared to let anything else interfere. Even if death interferes, that's only temporary. God oversees life and death . . . and eternity.

The disciples and the early church had an uncompromising mindset. They said, "We don't care if you persecute us. We don't even care if you kill us. We don't care what you do. We're going to obey God."

Whenever the body of Christ softens its commitment to God and begins to integrate humanistic concepts, it's no longer a church. It's a club, and clubs aren't run by God; they're run by committees.

Once when the scribes and Pharisees were criticizing Jesus' disciples for not following the traditional standards of ceremonial cleanliness, Jesus corrected them: "Neglecting the commandment of God, you hold to the traditions of men. . . . You are experts at setting aside the commandment of God in order to keep your tradition" (Mark 7:8-9, NASB).

Those religious leaders had identified something like 613 commandments from God in Moses' law, but by the time they had nitpicked through them all, they had arrived at more than two thousand. They had cited their own traditions for so long that they believed they were from God! How many assumptions have we made about God? How many ideas have we imposed upon Him? The Christian faith is about God's will, not ours. Jesus modeled that very truth in the Garden of Gethsemane which we will discuss more in Chapter 6. There is nothing wrong with praying for God to move in various situations we face, but there is something wrong when we assume that our own will in the matter is equal to God's. I want to obey God more than man, and I want to be led by God more than myself.

5) A forward-moving life must be with Jesus.

When we have a genuine encounter with God, it's like He puts a pin in that moment, so we'll remember it. How long has it been since you had a "pinpointed moment" with God? When's the last time you were on your knees in your prayer closet praying, "Lord, speak to me. I want to walk with You"? That's the kind of devotion that drove the people of the early church. The disciples might have been "uneducated and untrained" in the eyes of the world (Acts 4:13, NASB), but their confidence and knowledge made it clear they had been with Jesus. They built their lives on the absolute truth of who He is.

We can't build our lives on a shaky foundation. We can't put our faith in relative truths. There must be an absolute, or there's no way to measure whether we are decent men and women in the world. If you're trying to lose weight, the scale will tell you if you're going in the right direction or the wrong one. I can relate, because I love snacking and my weight scale won't let it slide. When I was younger, I could eat all the chips I wanted, but today, if I even look at a chip, my love handles will automatically grow. Matthew 7:24-27 tells us that the person who hears God's words and does them is wise like the person who builds his house on the rock (absolute). When the wind blows, that house stays standing, but the fool doesn't listen to God and builds on the sand (relative). When the wind blows, everything they've built falls, and it will be a *great fall.* Sin is a reality for us. People have told me, "I was just born this way," and I respond by saying, "That's why you need to be born again." The person who builds their house on the rock stays standing because they want Jesus more than they want compromise.

Hopefully, you can feel the confidence that comes with spending time with Jesus. Are you reading your Bible? Are you spending time in prayer? Are you moving forward past your mistakes or past your obstacles? Small victories lead to big ones, and it's quite possible that the miracle God is going to use to make an impact on your friends and your family is you.

CHAPTER 6

CHOOSING LOVE

Think back over your life and identify some things other people have done to prove beyond a doubt that they love you. Now, my love language is gifts, but for this exercise, gifts don't count—at least, not all of them. People can give gifts for all kinds of reasons. Sometimes giving a gift is mostly about making the givers feel better about themselves and has little to do with you. Sometimes the gift is for you, but

---

EASY COME. EASY GO. IT'S CULTURE'S IDEA OF COMMITMENT, AND IT'S BEEN COMPROMISED.

---

it's actually for them (the givers). For example, in the past, Lori has on occasion given me tools or a pressure washer. Anything used to fulfill a chore later on, does not count as a gift. Sometimes gifts have strings attached— so "you'll owe me one." However, if a gift is clearly selfless and sacrificial, you can count it. Make your mental list before reading on.

Okay, now that you have a list, identify *when* those loving actions took place. Are they evenly spaced throughout your lifetime? Are they mostly recent, or are your best memories of love clustered in your past?

‖‖

HIS LOVE FOR US IS A COVENANT, AND COVENANTS DON'T HAVE COMPROMISE.

‖‖

The reason I ask is that in my thirty-two years of pastoral marital counseling, perhaps the complaint I hear most often is, "We've just fallen out of love." I usually reply, "Well, you don't fall out of love like falling out a window," and then they clarify, "Yeah. But we once felt a flame of love, but now there's no fire."

Easy come. Easy go. It's culture's idea of commitment, and it's been compromised. Jesus compares His commitment to us (His church) as a groom who has sacrificed and laid his life down, for his bride. I'm so thankful He isn't a modern-day groom. He would have so many reasons to "fall out of love."

His love for us is a covenant, and covenants don't have compromise. Contracts do, though. That's the problem. We have misidentified covenants as contracts. Simply put, contracts are formed for each party to protect their own rights; whereas, in a covenant, two people surrender their rights and become one. We give ourselves for the other person. That's what Christ did for us, and that is why He designed marriage to be a display of the gospel.

Couples are challenged to keep the fires of love burning throughout a maturing marriage, especially in turbulent and unpredictable times. But every marriage begins with the mutual vow to love in sickness and in health, in wealth and in poverty, for better or for worse. All couples once (and for many, not so long ago), professed their spouse to be the greatest gift God ever gave them. It was literally "a match made in heaven," or so they thought. But now they want to return that gift, like a package from Amazon.

They started by whispering sweet nothings to one another, and now it's:

- "I never realized how much you were like your mother."
- "What's wrong with you? You can't open a door by yourself anymore?"
- "You're going out in *that*? Where are the Fashion Police when you need them?"
- "Flowers and candy? Wouldn't you rather have an exercise bicycle? You need that a lot more."

Some relationships die slowly in apathy and silence. Other couples find themselves distanced by increasing animosity toward one another. Sometimes the husband and wife simply pursue their individual interests until they discover a great gulf between them, and they realize they have very little in common.

This distressing erosion of love isn't just a problem with spouses. A similar decline in love can also occur in spiritual relationships. When most people come to Christ, it's with a sincere and passionate commitment to follow without questioning. We want to go where He wants us to go and do what He tells us to do. Too often, however, people lose that early momentum and may even wind up going in an opposite direction. What happened? What went wrong?

EMOTION VS. CHOICE

I think it boils down to the fact that love is a choice. If God so loved us while we were sinners, that same life and power is in us. Paul says, "If the Spirit of Him who raised Jesus from the dead dwells in you, He who raised Christ Jesus from the dead will also give life to your mortal bodies through His Spirit who dwells in you" (Romans 8:11, NASB). The same Spirit that raised Christ from the dead is inside you, so all believers should have the ability and the desire to love like Christ loved. That's why Paul reminds us that we have the mind of Christ (1 Corinthians 2:16).

One proof that love is a choice is that love is also a command. Jesus said, "I am giving you a new commandment, that you love one another; just as I have loved you, that you also love one another" (John 13:34, NASB). He also said loving God and others are the first and second greatest commandments (Matthew 22:34-40). Since Jesus commands us to love, He clearly expects us to love. Why would He ever command us to do something that we couldn't do? How foolish would that be? How cruel?

But Jesus didn't just command us to love one another; He *demonstrated* what love looks like. He showed that genuine love, God's love, involves much more than mushy words, flowers, and candy. In John 13, we read that Jesus, "having loved His own who were in the world, He loved them to the end" (John 13:1, NASB). John went on to describe how

Jesus, during their last meal together, got up, tied a towel around His waist, poured water in a basin, and washed His disciples' feet. It was a servant's job, but no one had volunteered to do it for the rest of them. Peter at first refused to let Jesus wash his feet, but Jesus said in verse 8, "If I do not wash you, you have no place with Me," and Peter relented.

GENUINE LOVE ALWAYS INVOLVES SACRIFICE, AND SACRIFICE OFTEN INVOLVES SUFFERING.

Afterward, Jesus said, "Do you know what I have done for you? You call Me 'Teacher' and 'Lord'; and you are correct, for so I am. So if I, the Lord and the Teacher, washed your feet, you also ought to wash one another's feet. For I gave you an example, so that you also would do just as I did for you" (vv. 12-14). The next day Jesus was crucified, and His devastated followers were left with this memory. Jesus' love was proven not through flowery words and token gifts, but through repeated acts of personal sacrifice.

As you recalled your own memories of how people have demonstrated love to you, I would predict that most if not all of them involved sacrifice on the part of the other person. Genuine love always involves sacrifice, and sacrifice often involves suffering. Love suffers. It hurts.

Only a short time after washing the disciples' feet, Jesus found Himself in the Garden of Gethsemane, preparing to demonstrate the depth of His love for humanity. He agonized as He prayed for a way to love without sacrificing, but then realized it wasn't possible and assented to His Father's will. He had already taught His disciples: "Greater love has no one than this, that a person will lay down his life for his friends" (John 15:13, NASB). The next day He went to the cross and showed the world the fullness of God's love. It was a gruesome sacrifice, but it was His choice.

Hollywood usually portrays love purely as an emotion—something that people "fall into" as music swells and birds sing. Early stages of love may feel like that, but genuine love must grow and deepen. When people don't hear the music anymore and stop feeling the purely physical attraction, that's when they come to see me, complaining that they've fallen out of love. And that's when I remind them that love is a choice.

Love means that you stick through every situation in every circumstance. It's not determined by whether or not your needs are being met at the moment. You and I don't meet God's needs all the time—at least I know I don't—but He still chooses to love me.

If we try to base love on physical attraction, we're in trouble. Those appealing physical attributes that you so admire are only temporary. That face, that hair, that body . . . it gets wrinkled, thinned, a bit heavy. You do what you can, of course. You work to stay as healthy as possible. After all, your body is the temple of God. But like Paul says, "Physical training is of some value, but godliness has value for all things" (1 Timothy 4:8, NIV). He says all that work we put into making our bodies look and feel better is profitable, but only a little. The approximate Greek translation is, "You're fighting a losing battle!" Regardless of your efforts, age is going to take a toll on that body, and that face that at one time you couldn't keep your eyes off of. Does that mean love has died? I hope not!

Very early in our relationship (before we were actually even dating), Lori and I were at a restaurant, and as we were sitting at the table, our attention was captured by an older (quite ancient, actually) couple. They were leaving the restaurant, hand in hand, looking admirably at each other. Probably if one of them had let go, they'd both have fallen. It was so sweet that, before thinking about it, I declared to Lori, "That's going to be us someday!" At that moment, Lori knew I liked her for more than a friend, and it also verbalized a vision based on commitment—not on looks, body, good teeth, or anything else that fades.

Peter writes that while it's okay to try to make ourselves attractive, we need to spend more time on internal attributes: "Your adornment must not be merely the external—braiding the hair, wearing gold jewelry, or putting on apparel; but it should be the hidden person of the heart, with the imperishable quality of a gentle and quiet spirit, which is precious in the sight of God" (1 Peter 3:3-4, NASB).

So . . . it's foolish and useless to base love on physical attraction. How about if we try to base love on feelings? We're still in trouble. Just think about it. How many times do your feelings change in a typical day based on what you're doing and who you're dealing with? Do you really want to base love on something so changeable? Emotions vary, and feelings fade.

It all comes back to the fact that love is a decision. Love is a choice. It's a conclusion. That's why married couples make a commitment, "until death do us part." And when children and friends and others come along, we can commit to love to them, even when they make decisions we might not agree with, even when they don't treat us as well as we think they should, regardless of what happens. When love is a decision, it can endure those imperfections of human relationships.

LOVE IN A BROADER CONTEXT

We've been looking at love on a personal level, which is where it should start, but as love grows, it becomes the glue that keeps the church connected to God and believers connected to one another. And just as love can fade between married couples, love can erode in church settings and create problems. John writes:

> *Children, it is the last hour; and just as you heard that antichrist is coming, even now many antichrists have appeared; from this we know that it is the last hour. They went out from us, but they were not really of us; for if they had been of us, they would have remained with us; but they went out, so that it would be evident that they all are not of us. But you have an anointing from the Holy One, and you all know. I have not written to you because you do not know the truth, but because you do know it, and because no lie is of the truth. Who is the liar except the one who denies that Jesus is the Christ? This is the antichrist, the one who denies the Father and the Son.*
> *—1 John 2:18-22 (NASB)*

John is writing about people who were once in the church, presumably followers of God in fellowship in the body. However, he says that they weren't really committed to God or the church to begin with. Otherwise, they would have stayed.

John wants us to consider: what was the difference between those who left and those who stayed? If they were part of us, how could they leave us? If we were supposed to be joined together in Christ and connected by His love—the same love that we all have experienced through the cross and the resurrection—how could they not just desert us, but turn against us?

The difference, he says, is that those who have remained "have an anointing from the Holy One." Anointing is a picture of baptism. What is this baptism, this power, that God's Spirit bestows? Paul tells us in Galatians. This fruit of the Spirit is . . . what? Not tongues. Not miracles. Not power. Not an experience. Not an emotion. When the Spirit of God is within you, it's *love*.

We need to make an important distinction here. Sometimes we say the *fruits* of the Spirit are love, joy, peace, patience, kindness, goodness, faithfulness, gentleness, and self-control (Galatians 5:22-23). But that's not exactly what Paul said. He wrote about the *fruit* of the Spirit as a singular, not a plural, term. He doesn't say, "The fruits of the Spirit are. . . ." No. He writes, "The fruit [singular] of the Spirit is . . ." and then lists those nine characteristics. We sometimes refer to the nine *gifts* of the Spirit, which is accurate, but what Paul was saying is that there's really only one primary fruit. There's only one reality of the Holy Spirit. And it is love . . . extended, multiplied, and amplified.

Love isn't one of nine equally weighted traits of believers. Here's how to look at what Paul is saying: Love extended is joy. Love extended is peace. Love extended is patience . . . kindness . . . goodness . . . faithfulness . . . gentleness . . . self-control. Love extended manifests in all these ways.

"Love" is perhaps the most misused word in the English language. One day I'm professing love for my wife, the next day for the Cowboys, and the next day for my favorite pizza. We've all probably told a crush at a young age, "I love you," when what we meant was, "I get butterflies in my stomach around you." That kind of "love" is here today and gone tomorrow. Hopefully, we eventually discover that genuine love remains firm and unmoving even when a loved one experiences a serious illness, a lost job, a financial crisis, or whatever.

AGAPE LOVE DEFINED

The Bible uses different words for "love," but the term to describe God's deep and lasting love is *agape*. And we would be hard-pressed to find a better definition than the one Paul provides in 1 Corinthians 13. No doubt you've heard this, especially if you go to many weddings, but let's take a closer look:

> *If I speak with the tongues of mankind and of angels, but do not have love, I have become a noisy gong or a clanging cymbal. If I have the gift of prophecy and know all mysteries and all knowledge, and if I have all faith so as to remove mountains, but do not have love, I am nothing. And if I give away all my possessions to charity, and if I surrender my body so that I may glory, but do not have love, it does me no good.*
>
> *Love is patient, love is kind, it is not jealous; love does not brag, it is not arrogant. It does not act disgracefully, it does not seek its own benefit; it is not provoked, does not keep an account of a wrong suffered, it does not rejoice in unrighteousness, but rejoices with the truth; it keeps every confidence, it believes all things, hopes all things, endures all things.*
>
> *Love never fails; but if there are gifts of prophecy, they will be done away with; if there are tongues, they will cease; if there is knowledge, it will be done away with. For we know in part and prophesy in part; but when the perfect comes, the partial will be done away with. When I was a child, I used to speak like a child, think like a*

child, reason like a child; when I became a man, I did away with childish things. For now we see in a mirror dimly, but then face to face; now I know in part, but then I will know fully, just as I also have been fully known. But now faith, hope, and love remain, these three; but the greatest of these is love. (NASB)

Everything we do on this planet is "in part." We never get the full picture. Specifically, we have a childish, incomplete concept of love. But as God works in our lives, we mature and leave those juvenile perceptions behind us. In fact, the Greek word for "did away with" means "ripped up by the roots." You don't root out your false beliefs unless you rip them out. We have to attack the shallow portrayals of what the world tells us is love. We're regularly inundated with these false concepts of love.

||||||||||||||||||||||||||||||||||||||||||||||||||||||||||||||||||||||||||||||||||||||||||||||||||||||||||

IT'S THE LOVE AND GOODNESS OF GOD THAT BREAKS DOWN OUR RESISTANCE AND CLEARS UP OUR CONFUSION.

||||||||||||||||||||||||||||||||||||||||||||||||||||||||||||||||||||||||||||||||||||||||||||||||||||||||||

When Jesus was at the Last Supper with His disciples, He knew He would soon face the cross and return to His Father. It was why He had come. As He looked around the table, we read that "having loved His own who were in the world, He loved them to the end" (John 13:1, NASB). It doesn't say they were in the church, or in the will of God. Scripture says they were "in the world."

They were still too worldly to understand what He was about to do for them. They still argued among themselves which one was the greatest. They were filled with confusion, questions, and misunder-standing. In the following hours, one would betray Him, one would deny Him, and all but one would desert Him.

Yes, they were in the world, but one theologian has said Jesus "loved the world right out of them." He loved their failures right out of them. He loved away their rebellion and disappointments. It's the love and goodness of God that breaks down our resistance and clears up our confusion. That's what it means that Jesus "loved them to the end."

The word "end" means "to the uttermost." The way we try to convey the thought in our terminology today is, "I love you to the moon and back." He loves us through all our troubles, questions, selfish concerns, and everything else. He patiently and mercifully waits for us to mature to the point where we acknowledge and appreciate His will for our lives. I recently heard someone say that the clearest definition of salvation is that *you love the will of God*. You can't say, "I love God," and still love the world, because loving the world isn't God's will.

GOD'S UNCOMPROMISING LOVE

This is God's mind about love. No matter what, He's going to love you, and He's going to keep loving you. It's a love without limit and without end. Let's look at some qualities of His magnificent love.

1) God's love is unending.

Nothing can stop God's love, so it never ends. The book of Lamentations was written during one of the most horrible periods of Israel's history, but right in the middle of the book we find one of the most uplifting and frequently quoted passages of Scripture: "The Lord's loving kindnesses indeed never cease, for His compassions never fail.

They are new every morning; great is Your faithfulness" (Lamentations 3:22-23, NASB).

Did you know you woke up to a whole new wave of God's love this morning? Do you detect His lovingkindness in this often dark and dreary world? Do you realize God has given you a new day to step into His love? I don't know about you, but the more I see going on in the world, the more I want to be sure I step into His love before I step into the morning paper. Perhaps you've felt that the world has taken the love of God right out of you, but God's love is inexhaustible. It won't stop no matter what.

God's love isn't hasty or incomplete like ours. Jesus loved His disciples through all their sin, through all their seasons. There's a lesson there for us. When we're thinking of making a major love commitment, like marriage, we need to consider all the seasons ahead. Maybe you meet in June at the beach, when you are both toned and tan, and you start considering a lifetime together. But you might want to reconsider in October, when the tan has faded, and you're not exercising as much. Still interested? If so, maybe you *are* ready to consider marriage. Either way, you'll know better after going through several seasons together before trying to rush love. It also takes practice and abundant forgiveness if you want *your* love for others to be unending. We're prone to put limits on our love. Peter did. He thought he was being quite magnanimous when he asked Jesus, "Lord, how many times shall my brother sin against me and I still forgive him? Up to seven times?" (Matthew 18:21, NASB) I think he was expecting Jesus to reply, "Wow, Peter. You are soooo holy!" Instead, Jesus countered with, "I do not say to you, up to seven times, but up to seventy-seven times" (v. 22). In other words, we tend to set our standards way too low. Our forgiveness should be like God's—unending.

I don't think the fire is the worst part of hell. The real misery is separation from God and His amazing love. When Jesus told His story of the rich man and Lazarus, He described how, after death, Lazarus was welcomed and embraced. The tormented rich man could see what he was missing but could never cross the great chasm that separated them. In this account, Jesus dispels any of our ideas that hell is a place where defiant and rowdy people will be happy and revel in the afterlife. Realizing what they've missed will fuel the deepest agony they've ever experienced. Meanwhile, believers will finally experience God's love in its fullness, without the barriers of sin that currently distort and confuse our experience of His love.

2) God's love is unconditional.

Jesus didn't just teach and preach about love; He modeled what love looks like. He taught His disciples to be servants, and then He got up from dinner to wash their feet. How could they miss the point?

"God demonstrates His own love toward us, in that while we were sinners, Christ died for us" (Romans 5:8, NASB). Jesus didn't wait until we could properly love Him back. We could never match His love. He died for us not knowing how we would respond. His love is unconditional: "When the kindness of God our Savior and His love for mankind appeared, He saved us, not on the basis of deeds which we did in righteousness, but in accordance with His mercy, by the washing of regeneration and renewing by the Holy Spirit" (Titus 3:4-5, NASB). His love isn't based on performing at a certain level, meeting a list of requirements, or anything else.

3) God's love is unmistakable.

Have you ever been fooled by romantic love? Maybe he told you everything you wanted to hear, and you were immediately head over heels. You replayed those (probably well-rehearsed) words over and over in your head every night before you went to bed. But when you got to know him better, you started to wonder, *How did those words come out of* that *guy?*

‖‖

GOD'S LOVE IS ALWAYS GROUNDED IN TRUTH

‖‖

Or she wrote the most beautiful letters when you first started dating. You waited expectantly every day for the next card or letter with that distinctive handwriting and just a hint of perfume on the stationery. Then, over time, they started coming further and further apart, until the letters stopped coming altogether. You thought it was love, but you had to think again.

We saw in the 1 Corinthians 13 passage that "love rejoices with the truth" (v. 6). God's love is always grounded in truth, as ours should be. Words alone aren't a sufficient indicator of love. It takes more: "Little children, let's not love with word or with tongue, but in deed and truth" (1 John 3:18, NASB).

Love always has to pass the truth test, and truth is more evident through our actions than through our words. Someone can say he loves God, and he can write that statement and sign it, but if he doesn't keep God's commandments or love God's will, the love of the Father is not in him.

Jesus warns us to be on the alert for false prophets. They are masters of deception, but He provides a surefire way to detect them before they do serious harm: "A good tree cannot bear bad fruit, nor can a bad tree bear good fruit. Every tree that does not bear good fruit is cut down and thrown into the fire. So then, you will know them by their fruits" (Matthew 7:18-20, NASB).

LOVE REQUIRES DISCERNMENT.

Don't be fooled. God's love always results in good fruit. People may show up at church declaring a great love for the Lord and His people, quoting the Bible, and professing to have performed many miracles. Some of them may even have fooled themselves into believing they are outstanding followers of Jesus, but one day, Jesus will tell the imposters, "I never knew you; LEAVE ME, YOU WHO PRACTICE LAWLESSNESS" (Matthew 7:23, NASB).

Love is more than feelings. Love requires discernment.

When you begin a relationship with someone, keep your eyes wide open. This is something parents of teenagers already know. One day the teen will come home "in love" with someone at school, but when the parents press for a few details, they discover their teen knows essentially nothing about the other person: family situation, work ethic, maybe not even the last name. The teen says, "Don't mess this up. You gotta trust me!" (If that's all it takes to mess up the relationship, I hope I do!) We need to hold those we love to a higher standard of accountability.

Of course, we often see faults in our children that we don't recognize in ourselves. If we find ourselves in relationships (friendships, business partnerships, civic commitments) that we shouldn't have been so quick to form, we need to hold ourselves accountable to God and make necessary corrections.

People frequently ask me, "What's it like living with a pastoral call? It must be like living in a glass house with eyes on you all the time." Sometimes they're even more direct: "Pastor Joe, we've been watching you!"

I tell them, "Good! Keep it up." I explain that what holds me accountable isn't all of their eyes—I'm aware that *God's eyes* are always on me. If I can live confidently in full view of Him all the time, then other people's views of me don't matter? God's love is unmistakable, and I want mine to be, too.

4) God's love is unpredictable.

What I mean by *unpredictable* is that when you love someone, you can't always predict what will happen. Don't we often do our best not to "waste" our love on someone who doesn't love us back? When it comes to love, we always want a return on our investment, but we never have any guarantees.

Jesus challenges us not to expect love to be a *quid pro quo* relationship. We may not know what to expect, but one thing we *shouldn't* expect is a one hundred percent return on our efforts:

> *"Give to everyone who asks of you, and whoever takes away what is yours, do not demand it back. Treat people the same way you want*

> *them to treat you. If you love those who love you, what credit is that*
> *to you? For even sinners love those who love them. And if you do*
> *good to those who do good to you, what credit is that to you? For even*
> *sinners do the same."* —Luke 6:30-33 (NASB)

These days it doesn't take opposing views on a great theological question or a differing comment on social media to cause division between believers. A political rift can do the job even faster. Love shouldn't be that flimsy! I understand the passion people feel and the lengths they go in support of their candidates, but when it comes down to it, are we to love only those who vote the same way we do? Or can we have a different position and still love those on the other side of the aisle? Of course, we can. We love others whether we get a return on that investment or not.

This was a classic demonstration of His parable of the sower (Matthew 13:1-23). When a farmer scatters seed, he knows there are many reasons why some of the seed won't germinate, but that shouldn't stop him from sowing and doing what he can. Jesus' point in the parable was the importance of spreading God's Word, regardless of the result. (More on that in the following chapter.) The same principle applies to spreading God's love despite its unpredictability. If we don't learn to do that among believers, what hope does our nation have?

5) God's love is unbeatable.

When we've experienced God's love, no other alternative can compete. We try money, possessions, fame, power, and sex, but those substitutes only create more problems. Solomon should know. He had all those other things, but he concluded: "Many waters cannot quench love, nor will rivers flood over it; if a man were to give all the riches of his house for love, it would be utterly despised" (Song of Solomon 8:7, NASB).

Again, change must begin with God's people in God's church. But it shouldn't stay there. It should flow from us into our businesses, our friend groups, our families, and our communities. I think our country is facing the problems it has today because there aren't enough people on fire with the love of God. In some cases, we have allowed the world to beat the love of God right out of us.

It's time to get up off the beat and rekindle that fire. Believers have the power of God within us. Jesus has set us free from the law of sin and death, so we can choose to be controlled by God's love rather than by the world or our emotions, feelings, or thoughts. If you've been looking for contentment in substitutes, ask God to renew His presence in your life. Put Him first again, and begin to love Him with all your heart, mind, soul, and strength. As soon as Christ becomes the number one priority in your life, your world will begin to make sense again.

CHAPTER 7

SOW FAR, SOW GOOD

The pandemic of 2020 will forever mark our memories—it was like nothing we've experienced in our history, and we all experienced it together. I want you to try to recall the first weeks when we heard the initial reports. The worldwide spread of COVID-19 was the first crisis of that type that most of us had ever experienced, and for many of us, it wasn't our finest hour. As panic spread, we desperately wanted to be in control, which is understandable, but the way many of us grasped for a sense of control was by hoarding. The availability of many items was sporadic for weeks. As soon as a shipment of frozen pizzas, eggs, bread, or other staples rolled in, the grocery shelves were quickly picked clean. But the item that was hardest to locate—it was like striking gold if you found it—was toilet paper.

On rare occasions, if the timing was just right, someone might have scored a mega-package of toilet paper at Costco or Sam's Club. I don't know if you happened to be one of those people, but suppose for a moment that you were. How did you (or how would you) respond? Would you hide every precious roll in various cabinets throughout your home? Or would you share the wealth with others? I told my "prepper" friends (the people who are always preparing for the end of the world) that they could either give me a roll of toilet paper, or I was coming over to their house.

As I approach the topic of this chapter, I hope you can see that in the days we're living in, it's our nature to resist generosity when times are hard. Most of us like to think of ourselves as loving and giving people, which we may be much of the time, but difficult times reveal things about us that are less attractive, less others-oriented. They expose our more selfish side. We become greedy and tightfisted. If we can get nasty over a toilet paper shortage, just imagine what we're capable of in a more serious circumstance.

There was a man in the Bible who found himself in a desperate circumstance. There were no Costco deliveries when there was a famine in those days. Isaac, who is a picture and symbol of the resurrection, was born into miraculous circumstances. His parents were way beyond their child-bearing years, ages ninety and one hundred. No doubt, Isaac's testimony in famine was shaped by a father who was called a "friend of God," a father who had riches but never had a permanent home. He chose to live in a tent, so he could quickly obey God's calling to other lands. His father even willingly took his miracle son, Isaac, to be sacrificed because God told him to, but it turned out (thankfully for Isaac) to only be God testing Abraham's obedience. God provided a ram for the sacrifice, but the act of giving up his son was a foreshadowing of what God would do later with Jesus. Extraordinary circumstances and supernatural occurrences surrounded Isaac's life. Now he found himself in another difficulty. Famine. I don't think any of us, even after enduring 2020, can fathom what it's like to not have food for ourselves or for our family, and not knowing when that could end. There was no end in sight. It might have months. It could have been years.

During the famine, Isaac decided to travel to Egypt (maybe because that's where his parents had gone when they were in a famine). We often resort to familiar, tried-and-true methods, going to places or things that have "worked before." But this wasn't the same time, this wasn't the same famine, and this wasn't the same person. God's future for Isaac didn't rest in Egypt, so God told him to stay in the place Isaac thought was just a pit stop.

‖‖‖

WE ARE NOT TO BUILD WALLS—BUT BRIDGES.

‖‖‖

The place was called "Gerar," which is the modern-day city called Umm. (I think that's comical—in English that's a "filler word.") Sometimes God leads into places that make us think, *Ummmm . . . God are you sure?*

This part of the story reminds me of a friend who went to minister for a "few weeks" in New Orleans, and he ended up pastoring there for more than fifty years. God sometimes pulls a "bait and switch."

Now, back to the story. Scripture tells us:

> *Now there was a famine in the land, besides the former famine that was in the days of Abraham. And Isaac went to Gerar to Abimelech*

> *king of the Philistines. And the LORD appeared to him and said,*
> *"Do not go down to Egypt; dwell in the land of which I shall tell*
> *you. Sojourn in this land, and I will be with you and will bless you,*
> *for to you and to your offspring I will give all these lands, and I*
> *will establish the oath that I swore to Abraham your father. I will*
> *multiply your offspring as the stars of heaven and will give to your*
> *offspring all these lands. And in your offspring all the nations of the*
> *earth shall be blessed, because Abraham obeyed my voice and kept*
> *my charge, my commandments, my statutes, and my laws." So Isaac*
> *settled in Gerar. —Genesis 26:1-6 (ESV)*

Gerar was an unlikely place. It wasn't what he would've picked. When God calls us to settle in a place, it's not to just exist; it's to invest. It's not to live alone; it's to engage with people. Having a generous spirit doesn't just revolve around our finances; it's also our friendships. We are not to build walls—but bridges.

Can I be really honest? If I had picked the place for us to plant a church, it wouldn't have been Austin, Texas. Don't get me wrong, Austin is a great place to raise a family, but I would've picked a place near the ocean . . . with much cooler temperatures in the summer. But like Isaac, God told me to stay here. I knew what that meant. We are all-in—ride or die!

The first place we went was the Chamber of Commerce. We were the first church to join, and we offered to provide pastoral care to their members. We even provided breakfast for their gatherings. Financially, this offer didn't make sense, because we could barely provide breakfast for ourselves, but we were sowing into our future. We were building relationships in the place where God called us to put down roots.

With no agenda other than to be a blessing, God began to build us as we sowed. God began to bless us with people who came alongside us and helped us build the vision God had given us.

We sowed into our neighborhood, hosting small groups and social gatherings in our small home. We sowed into area sports teams. We sowed into every person we met. Had I met you then, I would've taken you to Denny's or IHOP, where I showed up almost every morning, having breakfast with people when we didn't have offices.

||||||||||||||||||||||||||||||||||||||||||||||||||||||||||||||||||||||||||||||||||||||||||||||||||||||||||||||||||||||||||||||||

WE CAN GIVE WITH THE EXPECTATION THAT GOD WILL OUTGIVE US.

||||||||||||||||||||||||||||||||||||||||||||||||||||||||||||||||||||||||||||||||||||||||||||||||||||||||||||||||||||||||||||||||

We don't give (our resources/our talents/ourselves) to get, but we can give with the expectation that God will outgive us. Isaac modeled this for us:

> *And Isaac sowed in that land and reaped in the same year a hundred-fold. The LORD blessed him, and the man became rich, and gained more and more until he became very wealthy. He had possessions of flocks and herds and many servants, so that the Philistines envied him. —Genesis 26:12-14 (ESV)*

Isaac had experienced the resurrection power of God in a powerful way. He was spared death and received new life, but that didn't mean it was going to be problem-free from that point forward. He was still facing problems—in this case, a famine. Few of us will get very far in life without experiencing some kind of difficulty that strikes unexpectedly.

How did Isaac respond? He went where God directed him, and then he went to work. He began to sow.

|||||||||||||||||||||||||||||||||||||||||||||||||||||||||||||||||||||||||||||||||||||||||||||||||||||||||||||

IF YOU DON'T SOW, YOU'LL NEVER HAVE A HARVEST.

|||||||||||||||||||||||||||||||||||||||||||||||||||||||||||||||||||||||||||||||||||||||||||||||||||||||||||||

If you don't sow, you'll never have a harvest. It's a natural law. Isaac didn't sit around and wait for God to bail him out of every challenging circumstance, and we can't expect God to reward us when we shirk our responsibilities. Paul the apostle knew that law of nature, and he made it a rule for the Thessalonian church:

> For even when we were with you, we used to give you this order: if anyone is not willing to work, then he is not to eat, either. For we hear that some among you are leading an undisciplined life, doing no work at all, but acting like busybodies. Now we command and exhort such persons in the Lord Jesus Christ to work peacefully and eat their own bread. But as for you, brothers and sisters, do not grow weary of doing good. —2 Thessalonians 3:10-13 (NASB)

God has blessed us in so many ways. He has given us the ability to work and minds to invent and to create. We need to get up every morning and use those gifts for God, in whatever field He has called us. We need to respond to His blessings with a blend of gratitude and tenacity, not taking them for granted.

Most of us know that (and do that) when times are good, but we're still subject to our human nature that tells us that when we're in a famine, when we're not certain about the future, we need to hoard. We need to hold on to what we have.

I'm not talking only about financial matters. I'm talking about your talents and gifts. During seasons of famine, the natural response is fear, and the natural tendency is to freeze. But not Isaac. He took the seed he had and began to sow.

||||||||||||||||||||||||||||||||||||||||||||||||||||||||||||||||||||||||||||||||||||||||||||||||||||||||||||||||||||||||||||

EGYPT WILL BE ANYWHERE THAT'S OUT OF THE WILL OF GOD.

||||||||||||||||||||||||||||||||||||||||||||||||||||||||||||||||||||||||||||||||||||||||||||||||||||||||||||||||||||||||||||

I know the feeling of fear. When we moved to Austin, we immediately engaged in the community, but we weren't seeing the results I had hoped to see in the first year. We were plowing and sowing, but it takes time to see a harvest. Sometimes I would think, *God, did I mishear you? Did you say Boston, not Austin? Should we have stayed in our home state of Louisiana where we had friends, supporters, and options—and I had all my contacts from LSU?* But we knew it was purely human instinct to go back to what's familiar during a time of difficulty, so we resisted those urges.

Let me tell you, one of those options was incredibly difficult to resist. I had an offer from a very well-known church with thousands of people. The pastor contacted me and said, "Pastor Joe, I think you could be my successor here." We were in Austin, scraping and struggling, and I'll admit I was thinking, *You know, a man's gotta do what a man's gotta do!* But I also sensed God reaffirming to me, "You'd better not do anything except what I tell you to do." Enough said.

We saw in Chapter 5 that the faith of the Israelites departing Egypt was short-lived. They hadn't gone far before a problem came along that caused them to want to turn around and go right back. Even in my desire for security, I realized that any option other than God's will would have been Egypt for me and my family. For you, Egypt will be anywhere that's out of the will of God.

Isaac found himself in a time of famine. He followed God's leading to the unfamiliar land of Gerar, like we did in the unfamiliar land of Austin, and like many others who follow God into unknown territories and outside of their comfortable surroundings. When we encounter these times, we need to remember that how you *feel* about God's calling isn't as important as how you *respond* to it.

How did Isaac respond? He went to work. He began to plow. He began to sow. What did he have to sow? He had probably just a handful of seeds, but he sowed them instead of hoarding them. Then, before the end of the year, he reaped a hundredfold. Since the surrounding people envied him, it's pretty obvious that no one else was having that kind of success. Isaac was on track with God, and the Lord blessed him. He soon became rich, and eventually became *very* wealthy (Genesis 26:13).

Isaac had an abundance of grain, but that wasn't all. He soon acquired large flocks and herds, and a great household. In today's terms, we would say he had multiple streams of income.

I suspect that some of you are wondering at this point: *Pastor Joe, are you preaching a gospel of wealth?* I know other preachers sometimes make appealing promises that are not at all biblical. I'm not promoting those philosophies at all. But I *am* pointing to a biblical example in Genesis 26, showing that when someone obeyed God and then began to sow, even in a time of struggle, God blessed him with amazing success and greater influence. In Isaac's case, his success was measured with wealth and prosperity that included his whole household, but it wouldn't have happened if Isaac hadn't done exactly what God told him to do. Here's what I think we need to learn from the example of Isaac:

1) Keep hearing accurately.

Many of us have selective hearing when it comes to God's call. If He says, "Go to Hawaii," or "I want you to take this job that pays twice what you're making now," or "I have a beach ministry in mind for you," or something else appealing, we respond with enthusiasm. But if we hear any assignment that isn't appealing, or rewarding or that may involve a struggle, we become like kids playing outdoors when their parents are trying to get them to come inside for supper: "God, I didn't hear You!"

Our faith is rooted in our hearing accurately: "Faith comes from hearing, and hearing by the word of Christ" (Romans 10:17, NASB). Isaac heard God say, "Go where I tell you to go," but some of us see the evening news a lot more clearly than we hear the Good News. Faith comes by hearing the Word, so whose words are you listening to? I sometimes tell people I'm sick of the news, and they accuse me of just sticking my head in the sand. I tell them, "No, I'm not. I'm sticking my head in the Bible."

If I'm not hearing God clearly, I'm no good for my family. I have nothing to offer my congregation. I'm not a good friend. I'm a lousy neighbor. I'm no good to the Spirit of God because if I don't hear God correctly, I'll sow the wrong seed in the wrong place at the wrong time. "The one who sows to his own flesh will reap destruction from the flesh,

but the one who sows to the Spirit will reap eternal life from the Spirit"
(Galatians 6:8, NASB).

Some of the most powerful words that have fueled my purpose came
from my father when I was twelve years old. One day I answered the
phone when he called from work, and my dad said, "Joey, you have the
best speaking voice I've ever heard. You have a real gift of communication that's going to take you far in life!" Hearing my dad's encouragement has given me confidence to step onto any stage and speak.

||||||||||||||||||||||||||||||||||||||||||||||||||||||||||||||||||||||||||||||||||||||||||||||||||||||||||||||||||||||||||||||||

EVEN IF YOU DIE IN YOUR EFFORTS TO SOW FOR GOD, YOU STILL WIN.

||||||||||||||||||||||||||||||||||||||||||||||||||||||||||||||||||||||||||||||||||||||||||||||||||||||||||||||||||||||||||||||||

We have a heavenly Father who is speaking future into our lives
through His word. We need to be sure, especially in these days we're
living in, that His voice is directing our lives. You're going to have difficulties, struggles, and doubts, so you may as well plan for them. If
you're certain you've heard God clearly, you'll have His confidence
every step of the way through whatever you're facing.

2) Keep believing.

Isaac was in a foreign land, trying to avoid a famine, but he pulled
out those seeds and started sowing. He believed he was where God had
placed him. In the same way, we can believe what Scripture teaches,
that the character of the sower makes a difference:

> *There is one who scatters, and yet increases all the more, and there
> is one who withholds what is justly due, and yet it results only in*

SOW FAR, SOW GOOD   139

poverty. A generous person will be prosperous, and one who gives
others plenty of water will himself be given plenty. One who with-
holds grain, the people will curse him, but blessing will be on the
head of him who sells it. —*Proverbs 11:24-26 (NASB)*

Your belief will get you through even the hardest of times. Jesus said, "I am the resurrection and the life; the one who believes in Me will live, even though they die" (John 11:25, NIV). Even if you die in your efforts to sow for God, you still win.

Of course, I'm not suggesting we never grieve our losses. Death is sad. (But it's not just death: setbacks are hard, and family struggles make our hearts sick.) I get it. Jesus wept at the grave of Lazarus. My dad died in my early twenties. My mom died a couple years ago. I hated it. But what makes the passing of our loved ones a little less difficult is when we're reminded that God causes all things to work together for good to those who love God (Romans 8:28). For those who are in Christ, death is a victory. In time, we come to understand what Paul meant when he wrote, "For to me, to live is Christ and to die is gain" (Philippians 1:21, NIV).

3) Keep Being Willing.

The book of Isaiah, beginning in the first chapter, contains several passages that emphasize God's willingness—His desire—to bless His people: "If you are willing and obedient, you will eat the best of the land; but if you refuse and rebel, you will be devoured by the sword" (Isaiah 1:19-20, NASB).

God says that if you'll just do what He tells you to do, guess what will happen? You get the best of the land, but if you refuse and rebel, the sword will find you. I love the reality that God is a God whose word works, whether we choose to believe it or not.

Isaiah also confirms this truth about God:

> *"For as the rain and the snow come down from heaven, and do not return there without watering the earth and making it produce and sprout, and providing seed to the sower and bread to the eater; so will My word be which goes out of My mouth; it will not return to Me empty, without accomplishing what I desire, and without succeeding in the purpose for which I sent it." —Isaiah 55:10-11 (NASB)*

Isaiah says the Word of the Lord is going to do *something*, so it might as well be good. It's going to affect you in ways you can't even anticipate.

As our boys were growing up, Lori and I told them, "You can't get away from God's Word. You have praying parents, so God is going to give us insights into what's happening in your lives." They'll tell you now that there were many times Lori or I would call and say, "What's going on? There's just something in our spirit, and we feel there's something not right with y'all."

They'd ask, "How'd you know?"

And we'd say, "Because God told us, and we pray that you will always have an understanding that there is nowhere you can go to get away from Him or His Word."

People sometimes tell me, "Oh, I don't believe in God," or "I've been running away from God."

I hold out one hand, palm up, and tell them, "Maybe you're not in the center of His palm, but you're still in His hand . . . maybe over here on His pinky, or running toward His thumb, but He remains completely in control of your life." I explain that God operates like a fisherman. I tell them that people who have prayed for them have persuaded God to set a hook in them. God has always had to deal with resistant and defiant people but never gives up on us. He says, "I will put My hook in your nose and My bridle in your lips, and I will turn you back by the way that you came" (Isaiah 37:29, NASB).

A fisherman who hooks a fish first gives it a lot of line, and the fish thinks nothing of it. But as the fisherman sets the drag and begins to reel slowly, the fish realizes who's really in control. We can think we're running away from God, but He's just giving us some line. His hook is still in us.

If we love someone, we should even go to extreme measures to convince them to get right with God. One time Paul heard of a terrible act of disobedience in a church and instructed the church elders to "hand this man over to Satan for the destruction of the flesh." That's about as extreme as you can get, but Paul's desired result was "so that his spirit may be saved on the day of the Lord" (see 1 Corinthians 5:1-5).

4) Keep Sowing.

Nothing happens until you start sowing, and the number one principle of sowing is: "Do not be deceived, God is not mocked; for whatever a person sows, this he will also reap" (Galatians 6:7, NASB).

Going to church is an opportunity for sowing. Reading God's Word is sowing. You're investing time and energy that can result in a large harvest of spiritual benefits. You have to sow in the area of what you need. If you want to reap a financial harvest, you have to sow finances. If you need more time, you have to sow time. If you sow kind words, you reap kind words.

Sowing is a biblical principle that's active in every area of life. It sounds counterintuitive, but if you need an important job to be completed, you should assign it to the busiest person you know. These people have learned the law of time. A lot of people get touchy when we talk about finances in church, but Jesus often talked about money because love of money is the root of evil. If we're becoming more like Christ, we'll become more generous because Christ is generous. The supreme act of generosity is the gift of Jesus: "God so loved the world that He gave . . ."

Here are some great scriptures on generosity to live by in your personal, work, and ministry lives:

> *"The world of the generous gets larger and larger; the world of the stingy gets smaller and smaller." —Proverbs 11:24 (MSG)*
>
> *"A generous person will be prosperous, And one who gives others plenty of water will himself be given plenty." —Proverbs 11:25 (NASB)*
>
> *"Now I say this: the one who sows sparingly will also reap sparingly, and the one who sows generously will also reap generously. Each one must do just as he has decided in his heart, not reluctantly or under compulsion, for God loves a cheerful giver. And God is able to make all grace overflow to you, so that, always having all sufficiency in everything, you may have an abundance for every good deed." —2 Corinthians 9:6-8 (NASB)*
>
> *"Do not judge, and you will not be judged; and do not condemn, and you will not be condemned; pardon, and you will be pardoned. Give, and it will be given to you. They will pour into your lap a good measure—pressed down, shaken together, and running over. For by your standard of measure it will be measured to you in return." —Luke 6:37–38 (NASB)*

"In everything I showed you that by working hard in this way you must help the weak and remember the words of the Lord Jesus, that He Himself said, 'It is more blessed to give than to receive.'" —*Acts 20:35 (NASB)*

SOWING AND REAPING IN GOD'S TIMING

In 2004, I said to our church that I was believing God for one hundred acres on I-35. At that time, we were meeting in a six-thousand-square-foot industrial building on a potholed, hard-to-find road. But we were growing, breaking every safety code with our attendance, and adding more services—which was wearing us out! A couple in our church divinely stumbled upon a piece of land that fit the bill, but it wasn't for sale.

One day they knocked on the door of a little farmhouse on the land, inquiring about who owned the land. The man who answered the door said, "Who told you?"

They replied, "Who told us what?"

He invited them in and told them that his family (the owners of the property) had gathered to pray two days earlier about selling the property, which had been inherited from his father-in-law. As it turned out, his father-in-law, Mr. Barton, had bought this property in 1942. He was a man of faith who walked the property daily and dedicated it to the Lord. He believed that one day God would put a church on top of this hill (facing Austin) that would influence tens of thousands of people, a church that would reach the nations. He instructed his kids until his death in 1990, to preserve this land for the Lord's work. So in their prayer meeting, they asked God to reveal what church they should sell it to.

|||||||||||||||||||||||||||||||||||||||||||||||||||||||||||||||||||||||||||||||||||||||||||||||||||||||||||||||||

WHAT YOU SOW TODAY MIGHT BECOME YOUR
LEGACY FOR GENERATIONS TO COME.

|||||||||||||||||||||||||||||||||||||||||||||||||||||||||||||||||||||||||||||||||||||||||||||||||||||||||||||||||

Fourteen years after his death, a young pastor and his family from Louisiana came to this area with a calling that matched the man's vision, and the family sold us the land (110 acres, ten more than we requested) at a fraction of its value. That man sowed seeds of faith in 1942 that lay dormant for more than sixty years, but then came a harvest that now touches communities, prisons, and even other nations—a harvest that gets larger each year. People are now flocking to Austin from all over the nation, and many of them are finding God at this church that was only dreamed about until, in God's timing, it became a reality.

When you begin to sow for God, you may sometimes experience results so incredible you couldn't make them up. I know I have. Give God the opportunity to prove Himself to you, and who knows? What you sow today might become your legacy for generations to come.

CHAPTER 8
SOMETIMES YOU LEARN

We can all complete the sentence, "Sometimes you win; sometimes you (fill in the blank)." I believe there's another word that has much more insight and hope: sometimes you *learn*.

Most of what I've learned hasn't come from my years of formal education, or from my extensive library. (Full disclosure: My book-collecting addiction has caused more than a few marital disagreements.) I've learned through victories and setbacks. I've learned on the first time and on the fiftieth time. I don't believe we were meant to waste an experience, especially a failure, because we aren't meant to repeat them.

One failure that haunts me was that time I burned down my neighbor's garage—you read that right! I was an active and curious eight-year-old kid who got to go to a Fourth of July party with my eighteen-year-old brother. (Believe me, he wasn't thrilled.) I felt like I had arrived! You know there's always the neighbor who buys out the fireworks store, and people come from near and far to watch. And there

I was, a tagalong of an invited guest. Then I felt even bigger when my brother told me he was leaving to run a quick errand, and he left me at the party without him, warning me, "Don't you dare light anything!" I HAD ONE JOB. I completely intended to keep my word to my brother, but I just couldn't resist getting an up-close look at all of the fireworks—a garage full of them. Only, I didn't remember that I had a lit punk in my hand . . . that I then dropped. Then BOOM!!! Followed

WE ALL GROW OLDER, BUT IT'S A CHOICE TO GROW UP!

by endless booms! Everyone ran, and I ran away too, and then I thought I'd be clever and run back to the burning house, as though I was just coming to see it for the first time. That would fool them all! My brother returned at the time of my "come back." But, my brother took one look at me and knew the whole story.

Ever since that day, I'm abundantly cautious with fireworks. I can't see a sparkler at a wedding reception without remembering that experience. What if I'd taken nothing away from that terrible day though? Do you know that people get burned by experiences all the time, and then go on to put themselves in the same situations over and over to be burned again?

When the disciples were fearful on the boat, thinking they were going to die, it was just after Christ had multiplied the loaves and the fish and fed the five thousand. Jesus rebuked the disciples and said, "You gained no insight!" In other words, they should have grown in their faith from what had just happened, but they didn't learn anything about the ability of Christ to perform miracles.

We all grow older, but it's a choice to grow up! Even Jesus had to grow up in order to accomplish God's plan for His life! Luke 2:52 (ESV) says, "And Jesus increased in wisdom and in stature and in favor with God and man." If He had to grow, then we all have to grow! We never arrive. God needs us to never stop growing.

We often blame the devil for the difficult situations we are in, when it may just be God giving us a season to grow up. Whether a challenging situation is brought on by God, by the enemy, or by our own choices, God can take anything and everything and grow us out of it. He will bring purpose out of it. Romans 8:28 (ESV) says, "And we know that

|||||||||||||||||||||||||||||||||||||||||||||||||||||||||||||||||||||||||||||||||||||||||||||||||||||||||||||||||||||

STAYING BEHIND CAN GET YOU IN TROUBLE.

|||||||||||||||||||||||||||||||||||||||||||||||||||||||||||||||||||||||||||||||||||||||||||||||||||||||||||||||||||||

for those who love God all things work together for good, for those who are called according to his purpose." Not all things are good, but God works them for our good and for our growth.

King David, anointed and chosen by God, called "a man after God's own heart," in the lineage of Jesus—all of that, found himself in a situation that went from bad to worse . . . because he stopped when he was supposed to grow. "Then it happened in the spring, at the time when kings go out to battle, that David sent Joab and his servants with him and all Israel, and they brought destruction on the sons of Ammon and besieged Rabbah. But David stayed in Jerusalem" (2 Samuel 11:1, NASB).

Kings go out to battle. Kings expand and grow their territory. But notice, David stayed behind, and as I learned that Fourth of July, staying behind can get you in trouble.

Maybe David just didn't have the energy for another battle. Sometimes we've worked hard, and we need a break. Jesus took breaks with His disciples when they went on overnight retreats. We all need some down time, so we can recharge and be ready for the next big push. But getting away to reenergize is very different from playing hooky from your responsibilities, your God-assignment.

Early in his life, David was a picture of tenacity. From the time he was a shepherd boy fighting off lions and bears until after he killed Goliath, he captured the attention of King Saul, who became a fan, until he heard people praising David more than him. Then, Saul became jealous. It wasn't a passing annoyance—Saul was committed to killing the young hero! David and his "mighty men" ran from King Saul's soldiers in many dramatic encounters. Finally, Saul was killed in battle, and David became king. He was the consummate soldier, commander, and political leader. He was riding high!

Then, one day he sent his army out for battle, but he stayed at home. Maybe he was bored, or maybe he had some other excuse, but he wasn't where he should have been: at the head of his army. One day he looked out the window and saw a beautiful woman taking a bath on the rooftop next to the palace. The decision to stay at home and his boredom set some dangerous wheels in motion. He thought the unthinkable, conceived the inconceivable, and did what no one imagined he would do. Here's how the historian describes this sordid set of scenes:

> *Now at evening time David got up from his bed and walked around on the roof of the king's house, and from the roof he saw a woman bathing; and the woman was very beautiful in appearance. So David sent servants and inquired about the woman. And someone said, "Is this not Bathsheba, the daughter of Eliam, the wife of Uriah the Hittite?" Then David sent messengers and had her brought, and when she came to him, he slept with her; and when she had purified herself from her uncleanness, she returned to her house. But the woman conceived; so she sent word and informed David, and said, "I am pregnant." —2 Samuel 11:2-5 (NASB)*

|||||||||||||||||||||||||||||||||||||||||||||||||||||||||||||||||||||||||||||||||||||||||||||||||||||||||||

IT'S DANGEROUS TO STOP GROWING.

|||||||||||||||||||||||||||||||||||||||||||||||||||||||||||||||||||||||||||||||||||||||||||||||||||||||||||

Two words no man wants to hear from a woman who isn't his wife: "I'm pregnant!" David had to think fast. He sent for her husband, Uriah, to come to Jerusalem to meet with him, and David encouraged him to sleep with his wife, but Uriah refused to take liberties the other soldiers couldn't have. (And by the way, Uriah was one of the mighty men who risked his life for David, so the betrayal was even worse than it first appears.) So, without the neat solution of Uriah believing the baby was his, David had to go to Plan B: he arranged for Uriah, his friend and fellow soldier, to be killed in battle. The plan proved a bit messy when several other soldiers were also killed. So, here's what happened: the strong, noble leader who had grown so much as a man of God, had stopped growing, and his complacency opened a door for his calamity.

I'm not saying that every person who is in the wrong place at the wrong time will commit adultery, treachery, and murder, but I'm saying that it's dangerous to stop growing. We never can tell where our unfocused minds and hearts might lead us . . . and it's never to a good place!

||||||||||||||||||||||||||||||||||||||||||||||||||||||||||||||||||||||||||||||||||||||||||||||||||||||||||||||||||||||||||||||

LIFE CAN BE A GRIND, OR WE CAN GROW.

||||||||||||||||||||||||||||||||||||||||||||||||||||||||||||||||||||||||||||||||||||||||||||||||||||||||||||||||||||||||||||||

Learning isn't standard equipment for life's journey; it's an option we can choose or not. Life can be a grind, or we can grow. It's up to us.

Early in our time of pastoring Celebration Church, we decided to take a brief vacation to Lake Tahoe. At three hundred pounds, I was not necessarily in the best shape of my life, and I certainly wasn't an experienced snow skier. Still, I somehow found myself at the black diamond slopes. After literally crashing the entire way down the slope, I had a revelation (and a few broken ribs). I felt God say to me, "You can't do what I've called you to do at the weight that you are." I knew something had to change, and it was up to me. So, I changed my diet and began to exercise and just determined in my heart that I was going to stick with it no matter where it led. Within a year, I had lost seventy pounds and had a new energy to do what God has called me to do. It took failure to help me learn the lesson, but health continues to be a priority, and I have no desire to slow down pursuing all that God has for me.

I believe the principle is clear: most of us, most of the time, learn more from our failures, defeats, and wounds than from successes, victories, and acclaim. This is a hard lesson for many Christians who haven't advanced very much in their spiritual growth. When we read the Bible, we often see that setbacks set people up to learn extraordinary lessons.

WE OFTEN SEE THAT SETBACKS SET PEOPLE UP TO LEARN EXTRAORDINARY LESSONS.

Walking with God requires courage and tenacity. We begin as "babes in Christ," but if we're still drinking spiritual milk from a bottle months and years after we're saved, something is wrong. Yes, God is loving and gracious, but His grace energizes and compels us to learn, to grow, to serve, and to fight . . . not to stay behind or to stay immature. Grace is the green light to maturity and the motivation to live wholeheartedly for Christ. When we follow Jesus, we'll be challenged, stretched, and threatened . . . count on it!

Hebrews calls us to be strong and disciplined: "But we are not among those who shrink back to destruction, but of those who have faith for the safekeeping of the soul" (Hebrews 10:39, NASB). We're not passive—we're passionate. We're not timid—we're tenacious. We're no longer babes—we're brave. Let's get out of our baby beds and quit talking baby talk. (Lori and I didn't even let our *babies* talk baby talk!) It's time to grow up to the full stature of faithful and faith-filled children of the King. No more excuses. It's time to get moving.

To grow, we need to put ourselves in a training regimen, so we can learn more intellectually, go deeper with God spiritually, hone our skills so we can serve effectively, and develop endurance so we can follow faithfully.

||||||||||||||||||||||||||||||||||||||||||||||||||||||||||||||||||||||||||||||||||||||||||||||||||||||

GRACE IS THE GREEN LIGHT TO MATURITY AND THE MOTIVATION TO LIVE WHOLEHEARTEDLY FOR CHRIST.

||||||||||||||||||||||||||||||||||||||||||||||||||||||||||||||||||||||||||||||||||||||||||||||||||||||

NO PAIN, NO GAIN

Athletes have a distinct advantage in understanding the benefits of training. They know that pushing themselves to the limit makes them stronger, faster, and more resilient, and they're not the least bit surprised when they're exhausted at the end of a workout. That's what they expect! Grace introduces us to a life of faith and gives us a firm foundation, and we delight in God's grace and glory, but that's not all:

> *And not only this, but we also celebrate in our tribulations, knowing that tribulation brings about perseverance; and perseverance, proven character; and proven character, hope; and hope does not disappoint, because the love of God has been poured out within our hearts through the Holy Spirit who was given to us."* —*Romans 5:3-5 (NASB)*

That's the attitude of an athlete: Suffering is essential because it produces inner strength. Therefore, we welcome (we even celebrate!) hard times—not because they're so painful but because they're the classroom where we learn life's most important lessons. Paul, the personification of growing through suffering, made this statement towards the end of his life:

> *I have fought the good fight, I have finished the race, I have kept the*
> *faith; in the future there is reserved for me the crown of righteousness,*
> *which the Lord, the righteous Judge, will award to me on that day;*
> *and not only to me, but also to all who have loved His appearing*
> —2 Timothy 4:7-8 (NASB)

||||||||||||||||||||||||||||||||||||||||||||||||||||||||||||||||||||||||||||||||||||||||||||||||||||||||||||||

WE'RE NOT PASSIVE—WE'RE PASSIONATE. WE'RE NOT TIMID— WE'RE TENACIOUS. WE'RE NO LONGER BABES—WE'RE BRAVE.

||||||||||||||||||||||||||||||||||||||||||||||||||||||||||||||||||||||||||||||||||||||||||||||||||||||||||||||

I've had quite a problem with my vision in the past year or so, and the struggle has taught me a lot about my expectations and God's patience. I'm in good company, because Paul also had trouble with his eyes, and God used his difficulty to soften his heart and, paradoxically, give him a clearer vision of what's important. He explained that God used his suffering to humble him after He had given him special revelation:

> *Because of the extraordinary greatness of the revelations, for this*
> *reason, to keep me from exalting myself, there was given to me a*

> *thorn in the flesh, a messenger of Satan to torment me—to keep me from exalting myself! Concerning this I pleaded with the Lord three times that it might leave me. And He has said to me, "My grace is sufficient for you, for power is perfected in weakness." Most gladly, therefore, I will rather boast about my weaknesses, so that the power of Christ may dwell in me. Therefore, I delight in weaknesses, in insults, in distresses, in persecutions, in difficulties, in behalf of Christ; for when I am weak, then I am strong. —2 Corinthians 12:7-10 (NASB)*

SUFFERING IS ESSENTIAL BECAUSE IT PRODUCES INNER STRENGTH.

Paul learned that the benefits of rigorous spiritual training were so important that he delighted in the process.

Paul was writing to a church filled with people who had been acting like spoiled children. Again and again, he called them out on their pettiness and called them to follow Jesus in grace and power. Early in his first letter, he put the hammer down. Imagine getting this message from your pastor:

> *And I, brothers and sisters, could not speak to you as spiritual people, but only as fleshly, as to infants in Christ. I gave you milk to drink, not solid food; for you were not yet able to consume it. But even now you are not yet able, for you are still fleshly. For since there is jealousy and strife among you, are you not fleshly, and are you not walking like ordinary people? —1 Corinthians 3:1-3 (NASB)*

That's the point: If our hearts have been transformed by the love and power of God, we won't be "ordinary people" anymore! But we don't become extraordinary in a flash. Oh, yes, we're born again in an instant when we say "yes" to Jesus, but growth takes time, training, and tenacity.

Growth and maturity were very important to Paul. He knew the world wouldn't be reached with the gospel by Christians who couldn't find their way out of a crib. I believe he was the writer of the book of Hebrews, and like his message to the Corinthians, he took no prisoners. He launched into an explanation of Jesus being both the king and the high priest, and he pointed to the Old Testament story of Melchizedek,

||||||||||||||||||||||||||||||||||||||||||||||||||||||||||||||||||||||||||||||||||||||||||||||||||||

GROWTH TAKES TIME, TRAINING, AND TENACITY.

||||||||||||||||||||||||||||||||||||||||||||||||||||||||||||||||||||||||||||||||||||||||||||||||||||

who was both king and priest, as a model of Christ's dual role. But he realized his ideas were too advanced for their immature hearts and minds. He wrote them, "Concerning him we have much to say, and it is difficult to explain, since you have become poor listeners. For though by this time you ought to be teachers, you have need again for someone to teach you the elementary principles of the actual words of God, and you have come to need milk and not solid food. For everyone who partakes only of milk is unacquainted with the word of righteousness, for he is an infant. But solid food is for the mature, who because of practice have their senses trained to distinguish between good and evil" (Hebrews 5:11-14, NASB).

Really? They (and we) should all be teachers? Yes, without a doubt. A teacher doesn't necessarily stand in front of a class or on a platform. We teach our children about the love of God and right from wrong. We teach our friends what's most important to us by being an example to them. In every encounter, we realize we represent the Creator and King. We're His ambassadors, and our goal is to do everything we can to advance His kingdom. How? By communicating His heart and His purposes. That's a broader (and more accurate) way to think about teaching God's truth.

A MEASURING STICK

How do you know how much you've grown in your faith? What's a standard that gives you a good picture of where you are in your walk? We don't have to look far . . . the measuring stick is right under our noses. The words that come out of our mouths are the best indication of what's in our hearts. Jesus famously said, "Out of the abundance of the heart, [the] mouth speaks" (Luke 6:45, ESV), and James explained the principle in more detail:

> For we all stumble in many ways. If anyone does not stumble in what he says, he is a perfect man, able to rein in the whole body as well. Now if we put the bits into the horses' mouths so that they will obey us, we direct their whole body as well. Look at the ships too: though they are so large and are driven by strong winds, they are nevertheless directed by a very small rudder wherever the inclination of the pilot determines. So also the tongue is a small part of the body, and yet it boasts of great things. . . .
>
> With it we bless our Lord and Father, and with it we curse people, who have been made in the likeness of God; from the same mouth

> *come both blessing and cursing. My brothers and sisters, these things*
> *should not be this way. Does a spring send out from the same opening*
> *both fresh and bitter water? Can a fig tree, my brothers and sisters,*
> *bear olives, or a vine bear figs? Nor can salt water produce fresh.*
> —*James 3:2-5, 9-12 (NASB)*

Let me put it in my terms: When you get cut, what comes out? Do you bleed love and hope, or do you bleed resentment or despair? When we're under stress, when we're disappointed, when we've failed, or when someone has failed us, what are the words that come from our mouths? Do we curse or bless? Do we complain or give thanks? Do we blame or speak words of hope? The point about growth is that our words should (and will) change as we grow. As our faith is stronger, our love deeper, our commitment to God clearer, our words will increasingly reflect confidence in God's grace and His purposes for us.

TO KEEP GROWING . . .

Let me offer five recommendations to help you stay on track with God, so you can keep growing in your faith and effectiveness.

1) Take responsibility for your growth.

When I committed my life to Christ, I threw myself into God's Word, into serving, into being discipled. I felt like, at twenty-three years old, just finding Christ, I had so much to catch up on. We have to go hard after God. We have to be hungry to see His transformation take effect in our lives. Paul wrote the Philippians: "So then, my beloved, just as you have always obeyed, not as in my presence only, but now much more in my absence, work out your own salvation with fear and trembling; for it is God who is at work in you, both to desire and to work for His good pleasure" (Philippians 2:12-13, NASB). We don't work *for* our salvation, but we work it *out* as we say "no" to our selfishness and "yes" to follow Jesus wherever He leads.

We're not left alone to figure out how to follow Jesus. Paul told people that he was a role model they could emulate. "Be imitators of me, as I am of Christ," (1 Corinthians 11:1, ESV). Thirty-one years ago, I went to a pastors' conference, and a man I'd never heard of (because I was new in ministry) was preaching. I asked him to be my pastor. I have tried to imitate the life of Pastor Mel Davis for all these years. He's a prince of a man in every way, who is in his eighties now. I still call him almost every week. I never make a big decision without his wisdom, he gives me practical insight for my life and family and always amazes me with revelation from God's Word, that even after all these years, I've sometimes never heard. He has been one of the biggest secrets of my growth, especially in my early years of development. I had to initiate that relationship, and I have had to respond and be teachable in order to steward it. Whom are you following as you grow in Christ?

2) Be a lifelong learner.

I love to be around people who are always on the edge of new discoveries. They never stop asking questions, reading articles and books, and taking some risks to live life to the fullest. My son, Connor, is an avid reader, and if he isn't reading, he's watching documentaries. In fact, when he's home, it is like a 24/7 classroom—whether you like it or not. Sometimes, Lori and I say, "We don't want to learn right now, Connor!", and then he says, "But you just HAVE TO watch or hear this!" Can you imagine being one of Jesus' disciples, soaking in everything He said and did, and asking the questions the rest of us would love to ask as you sat around a campfire with Him every night? I'm sure they spent the rest of their lives unpacking all the insights Jesus shared with them.

The first thirty-nine chapters of Isaiah are about God's judgment for Israel's unfaithfulness, and the last twenty-seven chapters describe God's miraculous restoration of the people. At one point, God speaks through the prophet and makes this sweeping promise:

> *"Do not call to mind the former things, Or consider things of the past. Behold, I am going to do something new, Now it will spring up; Will you not be aware of it? I will even make a roadway in the wilderness, Rivers in the desert."*—Isaiah 43:18-19 (NASB)

Do you believe that God wants to do something new in and through you? He does. That's how I want to live—always asking, always reaching, always looking for God in every circumstance, always thinking about new ways to make a difference for Jesus.

3) Be resilient.

I know people who are stuck in the past. They messed up. They failed. They did something they're ashamed of. They hurt someone. They were terribly wounded by someone they loved. There are a million reasons to quit on life, give up on God, and fold our tents, but that only leads to more discouragement and disillusionment. It's easy to develop confirmation bias in politics. That's when we only listen to people who reinforce what we already believe. That can happen in our daily lives, too, when we listen only to the voice in our heads that says, "You're nobody." "You'll never amount to anything." "You're a loser." "You might as well give up."

A story in the Old Testament reminds us that it's never over. When God's people were surrounded by the Arameans, they were starving to death. Four lepers stayed by the city gates, and they realized they (and all the other people in Jerusalem) were in a hopeless situation. If they stayed where they were, they'd die; if they went into the city, they'd die. They decided to do something radical. One of them told the others, "Now then come, and let's go over to the camp of the Arameans. If they spare us, we will live; and if they kill us, then we will die."

||||||||||||||||||||||||||||||||||||||||||||||||||||||||||||||||||||||||||||||||||||||||||||||||||||||||||||||||||

ENCOURAGEMENT IS THE ROCKET FUEL OF SPIRITUAL GROWTH.

||||||||||||||||||||||||||||||||||||||||||||||||||||||||||||||||||||||||||||||||||||||||||||||||||||||||||||||||||

That night, they walked to the Aramean camp, but God had caused the sound of chariots and horses to scare the Arameans off, so the camp was completely empty. The lepers couldn't believe what they were seeing! "When these men with leprosy came to the outskirts of the camp, they entered one tent and ate and drank, and carried from there silver, gold, and clothes, and they went and hid them; then they returned and entered another tent, and carried valuables from there also, and went and hid them." End of story? No, not exactly. These four men who had been overlooked (at best) and mocked (at least), by their own people, realized God had given them an incredible opportunity. Instead of keeping all the loot for themselves, they went back to Jerusalem and told the gatekeeper and then the king about the deserted camp and all the loot. The king sent the army to investigate, and they brought back food, gold, clothing, and other things they desperately needed. (See 2 Kings 7:3-20.)

God used the imagination and courage of four very, very unlikely heroes to save the nation. If He would do that with them, what might He do with you if you show a little hope-filled tenacity?

4) Find a friend.

But not just any friend. Find someone who is a friend to your future, someone who speaks the truth to you, picks you up when you're down, and celebrates every success with you. Encouragement is the rocket fuel of spiritual growth. I would not be where I am without the friendships that God has placed in my life, and especially the friendship of my wife.

|||||||||||||||||||||||||||||||||||||||||||||||||||||||||||||||||||||||||||||||||||||||||||||||||||||||||||||||||||||||||

THE TRAJECTORY OF YOUR LIFE IS DIRECTLY RELATED TO WHOM YOU MARRY.

|||||||||||||||||||||||||||||||||||||||||||||||||||||||||||||||||||||||||||||||||||||||||||||||||||||||||||||||||||||||||

We have worked side-by-side for almost our entire marriage. We always say that the secret to our success as church planters, is that we never quit on the same day! When I was down, she was up. Or when she was down, I was up, and we encouraged each other to press on. Let me give you some marriage advice if you're single. The trajectory of your life is directly related to whom you marry. Choose wisely.

Your friends are also important to your success in life! We need people in our lives who believe in us . . . or more accurately, believe in God's vision for us. It's very easy to compromise when we're alone, lost in our own poisonous doubts, and susceptible to desires that lead us in the wrong direction. Who's talking you off the ledge? Who has hope for your future when it all seems dark? Who will you call at 3:00 in the morning when you're desperate for someone to help you?

You don't need a lot of those people, but you certainly need one or two.

||||||||||||||||||||||||||||||||||||||||||||||||||||||||||||||||||||||||||||||||||||||||||||||||||||||||||||||||||||||||||

COMPROMISE IS EASY; TRAINING IN RIGHTEOUSNESS IS HARD.

||||||||||||||||||||||||||||||||||||||||||||||||||||||||||||||||||||||||||||||||||||||||||||||||||||||||||||||||||||||||||

5) Keep your eyes on the horizon.

I know a lot more about ophthalmology today than I did a year or two ago, and I don't take vision for granted any longer. Eyesight lets us see what's right in front of us, and spiritual eyesight focuses our attention on the long view, the distant horizon where the fruit of our efforts today will become evident. The prophet Habakkuk asked God to give him a clear picture of Israel's future:

> *Then the LORD answered me and said, "Write down the vision And inscribe it clearly on tablets, So that one who reads it may run. For the vision is yet for the appointed time; It hurries toward the goal and it will not fail. Though it delays, wait for it; For it will certainly come, it will not delay long." —Habakkuk 2:2-3 (NASB)*

A lot of people have vague hopes for the future, but those who have a clear, compelling plan are far more likely to see their dreams become reality. When we write, we have to think carefully, write clearly, and consider the implications of each part of our vision. Do you have a vision for how God wants to use you? Do you at least have a vision for figuring it out? If you do, you'll almost certainly grow as you acquire the knowledge and skills you'll need to get there. If you don't, you'll drift from one goal to another, and finally, to no goal at all. I guarantee it.

IT'S A FIGHT

Those who aren't growing are easy targets—for random thoughts, for specific lusts, and for decisions they'll regret. I'm quite sure there's a direct correlation between people who gave up on growing and the wheels falling off their lives. Satan, Peter told us, is "a roaring lion seeking someone to devour" (1 Peter 5:8, ESV). In the wild of Africa, lions don't attack healthy animals. They look for strays and the weak. That's what Satan is looking for today . . . people who have strayed from God's path and are weak because they aren't growing in their faith. Jesus has defeated him, but people who are sluggish in their walks with God have lowered their defenses and given him an opening to attack.

Compromise is easy; training in righteousness is hard. The spiritual sweat of our training costs us some time and effort, but it prepares us to be all God wants us to be. Isn't that what you want? Sure, it is. That's why you've read this far in *Confronting Compromise*.

CHAPTER 9

THE WORTH OF WORSHIP

y good friend and leadership expert John Maxwell often says: "Everything rises and falls on leadership," which is very true. As a believer in the spiritual realm, everything lives or dies by worship. Effective worship is a prerequisite for competent leadership . . . and effective living on every level.

|||||||||||||||||||||||||||||||||||||||||||||||||||||||||||||||||||||||||||||||||||||||||||||||||||||||||||||||||||||||||

EFFECTIVE WORSHIP IS A PREREQUISITE FOR COMPETENT LEADERSHIP

|||||||||||||||||||||||||||||||||||||||||||||||||||||||||||||||||||||||||||||||||||||||||||||||||||||||||||||||||||||||||

So what is worship? It's something we all do. Everybody worships something or someone. Maybe only I notice, but I've been to concerts and sporting events, where everyone in the stands is doing what we do at a weekend worship service. They're clapping; they may be singing, they are raising their hands or their cell phones; they are making a joyful noise. I'm a loud, expressive fan in the stands of Tiger Stadium, so I'm not judging. It's a reflex—we were made to worship! But our greatest expression of worship was never meant to be for a ball going over an end zone line or into a basket, or for the most talented musical artists of our day. Our greatest act of worship is to be reserved for our God.

THE MORE YOU KNOW ABOUT GOD, THE MORE YOU'LL WANT TO WORSHIP HIM.

The more you know about God, the more you'll want to worship Him. And the opposite is also true: the less you know God, the less you'll worship. It's that simple. You know this to be true with human relationships. The better you know somebody who is kind, wise, and courageous, the more you appreciate them. The more time you spend developing your relationship, the greater your gratitude and love for them. That principle translates to our relationship with Christ.

Worship is important for many reasons, one of them being that it's going to be a part of our lives for eternity. It not only brings us closer to God for the rest of our earthly lives, but it also continues throughout our existence in heaven. We never stop giving God our worship and praise. Why? Because He gave His life for us. Worship is our ultimate response to the goodness and power of God. Worship is the ultimate reason for creation.God is certainly worthy of our worship. In fact, that's what the word means: worth-ship (like friendship). He is worthy of our praise, our thanksgiving, and our service. Even though He knows the awful things we've done (or still could do), He still chooses to love us.

Worship is giving God His rightful place (first place) in every aspect of life.

||||||||||||||||||||||||||||||||||||||||||||||||||||||||||||||||||||||||||||||||||||||||||||||||||||||||||||||||||||||

WORSHIP IS THE ULTIMATE REASON FOR CREATION.

||||||||||||||||||||||||||||||||||||||||||||||||||||||||||||||||||||||||||||||||||||||||||||||||||||||||||||||||||||||

"God is spirit, and those who worship Him must worship in spirit and truth" (John 4:24, ESV).

Worship is a combination of that which we believe by faith (spirit) and that which we live out in life (truth). In fact, our faith should motivate our actions.

IT'S NOT ABOUT ME

We've seen previously that Jesus, as He was preparing to start His ministry, was baptized and then was led into the wilderness to be tempted by Satan (Matthew 3:13-4:1). Satan knows the power of worship. Isaiah shows us that he was cast out of Heaven for declaring, "I want it to be about me! Not you, God!" (see Isaiah 14) The first church split happened over worship. Now after forty days in the wilderness, Jesus was very hungry, so the devil tried to convince Him to turn stones into bread. Have you ever made some bad decisions in life when you were really hungry? But Jesus wouldn't compromise, and quoted Scripture to defend His response. Next, the devil attempted to get Him to throw Himself off the pinnacle of the temple and trust the angels to keep Him from being harmed. Again, Jesus quoted Scripture and wasn't swayed by Satan's tactic. Finally, the devil tried a temptation that has worked on many people throughout history:

> *Again, the devil took Him to a very high mountain and showed Him*
> *all the kingdoms of the world and their glory; and he said to Him,*
> *"All these things I will give You, if You fall down and worship*
> *me." —Matthew 4:8-9 (NASB)*

Since the beginning, people have been tempted to seek their own glory, but Jesus didn't take the bait. Satan was appealing to the self-centered nature of Jesus but soon realized that there was no self-centered nature in Jesus. Jesus lived to give glory to the Father, and He did so through His humility and conviction. Whenever we're being tempted,

||||||||||||||||||||||||||||||||||||||||||||||||||||||||||||||||||||||||||||||||||||||||||||||||||||||||||||||

THE WORST THING YOU CAN DO IS STOP WORSHIPING GOD.

||||||||||||||||||||||||||||||||||||||||||||||||||||||||||||||||||||||||||||||||||||||||||||||||||||||||||||||

the first thing to remember is that Satan is a liar (John 8:44). Just because he says he's going to do something doesn't necessarily mean that he will . . . or that he can. And the next thing we need to remember is what Jesus told the devil in response: "Go away, Satan! For it is written: 'YOU SHALL *WORSHIP* THE LORD YOUR GOD, AND SERVE HIM ONLY'" (Matthew 4:10, NASB, emphasis added).

Regardless of the battles you're fighting, the problems you're trying to resolve, or the temptations you're facing, the worst thing you can do is stop worshiping God. He's our unending source of life, health, and joy. If Satan can get you to take your eyes off God and shift your worship to money, prestige, possessions, pleasure, or comfort, he's got you. Jesus, the Son of God, knew who His Father was. As soon as Jesus started dropping scriptural bombs on the devil, the Bible says, "Then the devil left him; and behold, angels came and began to serve Him" (Matthew 4:11, NASB). Satan could no longer remain in His presence.

WE WORSHIP GOD WHEN WE HONOR HIM IN ALL THINGS, ALL DAY, EVERY DAY.

The Bible says to "rejoice always" and "pray without ceasing" (see 1 Thessalonians 5:16-17). I also think it's appropriate to read that as "worship always" and "worship without ceasing." Our worship should be continuous, nonstop, an ongoing part of our lives—because worship isn't confined to an hour on Sunday mornings or a block of time every day. We worship God when we honor Him in all things, all day, every day.

Worship is the ultimate issue of the universe. It's the most important thing that you will ever understand. It's the reason for your existence; it's your purpose. As we've just seen in Matthew 4, it's the catalyst for the ultimate war. When you look beneath the surface of all today's conflicts, you discover they all involve worship—or more accurately, the lack of it.

Worship is the ultimate theme of the Bible. No matter what you read, Old Testament or New Testament, you'll find the same questions showing up: Whom are you going to worship? Whom will you give glory to?

Worship is the ultimate issue of the church. Worship is our purpose as individual believers and as a body, and this chapter will examine how we should make that truth a reality.

IIIIIIIIIIIIIIIIIIIIIIIIIIIIIIIIIIIIIIIIIIIIIIIIIIIIIIIIIIIIIIIIIIIIIIIIIIIIIIIIIIIIIIIIIIIIIIIIIIIIIIIIIIIIIIIIIIIII

WORSHIP IS THE ULTIMATE, THE PRIORITY, THE PINNACLE OF GOD'S EXPECTATIONS FOR HIS PEOPLE.

IIIIIIIIIIIIIIIIIIIIIIIIIIIIIIIIIIIIIIIIIIIIIIIIIIIIIIIIIIIIIIIIIIIIIIIIIIIIIIIIIIIIIIIIIIIIIIIIIIIIIIIIIIIIIIIIIIIII

First you might ask why I consider worship to be *ultimate*. It's ultimate because God said it is. As He was preparing to give His people the Ten Commandments, He told them:

> *"I am the Lord your God, who brought you out of the land of Egypt, out of the house of slavery. You shall have no other gods before Me. You shall not make for yourself an idol, or any likeness of what is in heaven above or on the earth beneath, or in the water under the earth. You shall not worship them nor serve them; for I, the Lord your God, am a jealous God, inflicting the punishment of the fathers on the children, on the third and the fourth generations of those who hate Me, but showing favor to thousands, to those who love Me and keep My commandments."* —Exodus 20:2-6 (NASB)

The first two commandments center around worship. Worship is the ultimate, the priority, the pinnacle of God's expectations for His people. This awareness needs to be anchored in your faith and in every aspect of your life. I do believe, if you are uncomfortable with the idea of worship, it's probably because you may need a clearer understanding about what it means to be a worshiper.

WHEN THE HEAT IS ON

What I think is perhaps the most relevant and uncompromising example of commitment to worship God is the biblical story of Shadrach, Meshach, and Abednego in the book of Daniel. The three had been taken captive to Babylon along with Daniel. God had blessed them in that foreign land and enabled them to rise in the ranks despite a lot of competent competition. We saw Daniel's lions' den challenge several chapters ago, but he must have been out of town for what happened to his three friends.

|||||||||||||||||||||||||||||||||||||||||||||||||||||||||||||||||||||||||||||||||||||||||||||||||||||||

NOT ALL IDOLS ARE MADE OF GOLD AND SITTING IN TEMPLES.

|||||||||||||||||||||||||||||||||||||||||||||||||||||||||||||||||||||||||||||||||||||||||||||||||||||||

King Nebuchadnezzar was ruling Babylon at the time, and one day he decided *he* deserved some worship. He made a golden image representing himself, ninety feet tall, and set it up on a plain so it could be seen by everyone. He then ordered all his officials at every level and all his subjects to assemble for the dedication of the image. He explained that music was about to play, and that would be the signal for everyone in attendance to bow down and worship the gold statue. As an incentive, he said that anyone who failed to do so would be immediately thrown into a blazing furnace. (Quite an incentive to worship!)

Not all idols are made of gold and sitting in temples. Not all idols are "bad" in and of themselves. They are just things out of the proper priority. I had never known a life without football. If I was not playing it, I was watching it. One day I realized that everything centered around it: my schedule, my money, and almost all of my conversation. It was stealing my focus and energy. It had become an idol, and I knew something needed to change. So, I committed to God that I would take it out of my life until I was certain that God was first place for me—that ended up being about five years!

You turn from idols to worship God. In fact, the first stage in Christian faith is to turn to God. This is a repeated test. When God convicts us to change something in our lives, we should ask, "Is Jesus worth this?" It realigns us quickly to what matters most. So the music started to play, and when they heard it, all the people bowed to the golden image. No doubt many of them had no intention of actually worshiping the statue, but everyone bowed rather than risk the wrath of a powerful and temperamental king—everyone except for three young men from Judea.

Whenever people who have an unpopular viewpoint refuse to go along with the crowd, someone usually gets upset. In this case, a group of Chaldeans (some translations say "astrologers") went to Nebuchadnezzar to rat out Shadrach, Meshach, and Abednego. They played to the king's ego as they trash-talked the three Jews.

Nebuchadnezzar responded "in rage and anger" as he summoned the three. But they were valuable assets to him, so he explained the instructions again and offered them a second chance to bow.

> *"Now if you are ready, at the moment you hear the sound of the horn, flute, lyre, trigon, psaltery and bagpipe, and all kinds of musical instruments, to fall down and worship the statue that I have made, very well. But if you do not worship, you will immediately be thrown into the midst of a furnace of blazing fire; and what god is there who can rescue you from my hands?"*
>
> *Shadrach, Meshach, and Abednego replied to the king, "Nebuchadnezzar, we are not in need of an answer to give you concerning this matter. If it be so, our God whom we serve is able to rescue us from the furnace of blazing fire; and He will rescue us from your hand, O king. But even if He does not, let it be known to you, O king, that we are not going to serve your gods nor worship the golden statue that you have set up."* —Daniel 3:15-18 (NASB)

They weren't going to compromise. They believed their God could deliver them if He wanted, but even if He didn't, they weren't going to worship any other gods.

Nebuchadnezzar was so filled with wrath that his face became contorted (v. 19). He had the furnace cranked up to seven times its usual heat. (The Hebrew translation means "Texas in July hot!") In fact, it became so hot that it killed the soldiers who tossed the three friends, bound, into the furnace.

Lesson learned. No one defies the king of Babylon. It was the end of the story, until it wasn't. It was actually Nebuchadnezzar who had a lesson to learn. He looked into the furnace and was "astounded" for several reasons. For one thing, the guys in the furnace were up and walking around in the fire, unharmed. For another (and he asked for clarification about this one), they had only thrown in the three Hebrews who refused to bow to the statue, but now there were *four* figures in the flames, and the fourth one, in his words, "Looks like the Son of God!" (see vv. 24-25)

It's amazing. In this Old Testament account, hundreds of years before Christ would come, Nebuchadnezzar saw Jesus in the fire. It was a Christophany, an appearance of Christ. The king had a front row seat to the power of God, and it changed his tune. The king suddenly realized that Shadrach, Meshach, and Abednego were "servants of the

||||||||||||||||||||||||||||||||||||||||||||||||||||||||||||||||||||||||||||||||||||||||||||||||||||||||||||

THE WAY WE WORSHIP GOD IN TRIALS, OR IN PAIN, SPEAKS LOUDLY TO THOSE WHO ARE WATCHING.

||||||||||||||||||||||||||||||||||||||||||||||||||||||||||||||||||||||||||||||||||||||||||||||||||||||||||||

Most High God," and he called them to come out of the fire. All the assembled dignitaries confirmed that the fire had done no bodily harm to the three. Not only that, but they didn't have a singed hair on them, and they didn't even smell like smoke. Nebuchadnezzar made an official proclamation in Daniel 6:28-30 that anyone who spoke against the God of these three friends would be torn limb from limb. Ouch. Notice that Christ did not show up until after they were in the fire. The way we worship God in trials, or in pain, speaks loudly to those who are watching.

Centuries later, as the author of Hebrews reflected on all the Old Testament heroes of faith and the many ways God had acted on their behalf, he must have been thinking about the book of Daniel as he wrote that some, by faith, had "shut the mouths of lions" and "quenched the power of fire" (see Hebrews 11:33-34). Then, in the following chapter, he challenges us: "Therefore, since we receive a kingdom which cannot be shaken, let's show gratitude, by which we may offer to God an acceptable service with reverence and awe; for our God is a consuming fire" (Hebrews 12:28-29, NASB).

Because Shadrach, Meshach, and Abednego worshiped a God whose kingdom couldn't be shaken, they had no fear of Nebuchadnezzar's fire. The fiery furnace was only a pilot light, a Bic lighter, a mild sunburn compared to the eternal, consuming fire of the God they served. After we've experienced God's fire, we have no fear of the heat generated by Satan's lies.

||||||||||||||||||||||||||||||||||||||||||||||||||||||||||||||||||||||||||||||||||||||||||||||||||||||

WHEN YOU STAND TALL, YOU STAND OUT.

||||||||||||||||||||||||||||||||||||||||||||||||||||||||||||||||||||||||||||||||||||||||||||||||||||||

STILL STANDING FIRM

I believe the world is in a moment much like the one experienced by Shadrach, Meshach, and Abednego. When you stand tall for God in a culture where most others are bowing down to various gods of money, status, sex, pleasure, and power, people are going to notice. When you stand tall, you stand out. Some are going to question you, perhaps even threaten you, and probably cancel you. But when we worship God, He wants us to worship all the time, whether others are watching or not.

When young people go to college, they're often advised to keep an open mind. That's terrible advice. If I've already met the living and true God, I don't open my mind to any other so-called "truths." I don't open my mind to any other commandments. I don't open my mind to any other savior, any other Lord. I open my mind and heart to God's Word.

When young adults go into the workplace or some social setting, they sometimes feel enormous pressure to fit in, to be one of the crowd. But how far are you willing to go to conform? Do you overindulge at the open bar because everyone else does? Do you let a racist joke go by

|||||||||||||||||||||||||||||||||||||||||||||||||||||||||||||||||||||||||||||||||||||||||||||||||||||||||||||||||||||||||||

WHEN YOU STAND FOR YOUR CONVICTIONS, THE WORLD WANTS YOU TO FEEL SMALL

|||||||||||||||||||||||||||||||||||||||||||||||||||||||||||||||||||||||||||||||||||||||||||||||||||||||||||||||||||||||||||

because everyone is laughing? It's so easy to compromise our faith and morals to be accepted. The young adults in this story felt the pressure to bow. They were made to look ridiculous and out of touch because everyone else was bowing. How could they go against what every cultural icon and politician was saying about the golden statue? When you stand for your convictions, the world wants you to feel small, singled out, and shamed. But Jesus has made it clear that His followers aren't of this world: "If you were of the world, the world would love you as its own; but because you are not of the world, but I chose you out of the world, because of this the world hates you" (John 15:19, NASB).

LETTER-PERFECT WORSHIP

It all comes down to this: Whose god are you going to worship? You have lots of options, but only one is the true and living God. I've created an acronym using the word WORSHIP to help us keep our focus where it belongs: on God and God alone.

Why we exist

God told Isaiah He would "bring My sons from afar and My daughters from the ends of the earth, everyone who is called by My name, and whom I have created for My glory, whom I have formed, even whom I have made" (Isaiah 43:6-7, NASB). God has created you for His glory.

We're reminded throughout the Psalms that all creation exists to draw attention to God and to invoke our worship:

> *"The heavens tell of the glory of God; and their expanse declares the work of His hands." —Psalm 19:1 (NASB)*
>
> *"For the Lord is a great God and a great King above all gods, in whose hand are the depths of the earth, the peaks of the mountains are also His. The sea is His, for it was He who made it, and His hands formed the dry land. Come, let's worship and bow down, let's kneel before the Lord our Maker. For He is our God." —Psalm 95:3-7 (NASB)*
>
> *"Let everything that has breath praise the LORD." —Psalm 150:6 (NIV).*

Shadrach, Meshach, and Abednego understood Who that fourth man was in the fire with them. It was Christ. Today, we need to more readily acknowledge Christ in our presence:

> *Have this attitude in yourselves which was also in Christ Jesus, who, as He already existed in the form of God, did not consider equality*

*with God something to be grasped, but emptied Himself by taking
the form of a bond-servant and being born in the likeness of men.
And being found in appearance as a man, He humbled Himself by
becoming obedient to the point of death: death on a cross. For this
reason also God highly exalted Him, and bestowed on Him the name
which is above every name, so that at the name of Jesus every knee
will bow, of those who are in heaven and on earth and under the
earth, and that every tongue will confess that Jesus Christ is Lord,
to the glory of God the Father.* —*Philippians 2:5-11 (NASB)*

I believe that's what those three guys were doing in the fiery furnace.
Even in the Old Testament, they were giving glory to Jesus, because
they knew that He had made them. He had created them not only for
relationship, but also for worship and for praise.

WHEN YOU WORSHIP, IT CAUSES THE DOORS OF HEAVEN TO OPEN.

Open doors

When you worship, it causes the doors of heaven to open. Even in the
furnace, the heavens opened for Shadrach, Meshach, and Abednego,
and Jesus was in the midst of the fire with them.

When Solomon had completed the temple, the priests brought in the
ark and positioned it in the Most Holy Place. The ark would symbolize
God's presence among them, but on this day His presence was even
more evident. The people were praising and glorifying God with songs

and many instruments, saying "He indeed is good, for His kindness is everlasting." As they did, a holy cloud filled the building to the point where the priests couldn't even stand to minister. The presence of God opened over them (see 2 Chronicles 5). That's what happens in worship.

In Acts 16:25-26, when Paul and Silas were in prison for preaching the gospel, they were praying and singing hymns to God at midnight as the other prisoners listened. In response to their worship, a great earthquake shook the foundations of that prison. Immediately all the cell doors were opened, and everyone's chains were unfastened. It was no coincidence; it was worship. Worship breaks the chains of bondage and opens the heavens.

|||||||||||||||||||||||||||||||||||||||||||||||||||||||||||||||||||||||||||||||||||||||||||||||||||||||||||||||||||||

WHEN WE SET OUR ATTENTION ON GOD THROUGH WORSHIP, THINGS BEGIN TO CHANGE.

|||||||||||||||||||||||||||||||||||||||||||||||||||||||||||||||||||||||||||||||||||||||||||||||||||||||||||||||||||||

Renews our spirit and body

Do you ever go somewhere for a spa treatment? If you've been overworked or overstressed, sometimes you need to be renewed in your body and mind. Someone starts to massage out those tight spots as you listen to soothing music and breathe in a refreshing aroma. It makes a difference.

Well, every time you worship, it's like going for a spa treatment where your spirit is renewed. It forces out the tensions and troubles of the world and centers your mind on God. It renews you.

Paul wrote,

> *I urge you, brothers and sisters, by the mercies of God, to present your bodies as a living and holy sacrifice, acceptable to God, which is your spiritual service of worship. And do not be conformed to this world, but be transformed by the renewing of your mind, so that you may prove what the will of God is, that which is good and acceptable and perfect.* —*Romans 12:1-2 (NASB)*

|||||||||||||||||||||||||||||||||||||||||||||||||||||||||||||||||||||||||||||||||||||||||||||||||

WORSHIP EMPOWERS AND ELEVATES YOU.

|||||||||||||||||||||||||||||||||||||||||||||||||||||||||||||||||||||||||||||||||||||||||||||||||

In other words, get your body into the presence of God. When we set our attention on God through worship, things begin to change. Let His Spirit renew your mind. You will find that God can give you a brand new perspective. Those young Hebrew men knew they were in the will of God. They weren't going to bow to any other gods, because they were filled with the presence of the true God. Even if death was going to be in their future, they were in the hand of God. He would deliver them—one way or another.

Spiritual warfare

Worship empowers and elevates you. The war we wage is not against flesh and blood; there is a spiritual enemy who is in complete opposition to the ways of God. Worship is a weapon against the devil. I have seen people find breakthrough in their lives in one moment of worship that they couldn't find in years of counseling. I agree that Christian counseling is beneficial, but I also know God responds to worship.

We're all in a battle. On a personal level, what struggles have you experienced lately, either physical or spiritual? We know Satan wants to kill, steal, and destroy, so we must resist him. The Bible says we are to endure hardship as a good soldier (2 Timothy 2:3), and the greatest weapon at our disposal is worship. Give God praise. Give Him glory. That's what Shadrach, Meshach, and Abednego did. You may have a child who is far from God . . . keep worshiping. You may have received a diagnosis that has shaken your entire world . . . keep worshiping. It is our response, and it is our weapon. It reminds us of the faithfulness of God.

At one point in their history, Judah was being invaded by a coalition of their enemies—in fact, a great multitude of them. God told King Jehoshaphat to march against them, and to put the singers out in front! It must have sounded like a terrible battle plan to a lot of people, but

GENUINE WORSHIP CONNECTS THE WORSHIPER WITH CHRIST.

the singers were worshiping and singing, "Give thanks to the Lord, for His faithfulness is everlasting." And as the opposing armies got closer to each other, the Lord set ambushes against the enemies of Judah, and they ended up completely destroying themselves (2 Chronicles 20:20-23, NASB). When you worship God, He routs your enemies—whoever and wherever they are.

Has no compromise

We see that Daniel and his three friends consistently worshiped God, and therefore, they never compromised. They demonstrated that there was a difference between genuine worship and false worship. The difference has to do with motivations.

Genuine worship connects the worshiper with Christ. God told Amos, "Take away from Me the noise of your songs; I will not even listen to the sound of your harps. But let justice roll out like waters, and righteousness like an ever-flowing stream" (Amos 5:23-24, NASB). In other words, "You don't really love Me. You don't really care for Me. You're just using Me to get what you want." We need to be careful about reading the Bible or going to God to get what we want rather than to give Him the worship and honor He deserves. Do we find God to be only useful, or do we find Him to be good because of who He is? If you worship God for who He is, He will do what He does.

‖‖‖

WHEN YOU'RE IN THE FIRE, GOD HAS YOU COVERED.

‖‖‖

Insulates us from the fire

Times will come when we all will face the fire. Peter warns, "Beloved, do not be surprised at the fiery ordeal among you, which comes upon you for your testing, as though something strange were happening to you; but to the degree that you share the sufferings of Christ, keep on rejoicing, so that at the revelation of His glory you may also rejoice and be overjoyed" (1 Peter 4:12-13, NASB).

What do you do when you're in the fire? You keep on rejoicing; you worship! When you're in the fire, God has you covered. When the Lord was in the furnace with Shadrach, Meshach, and Abednego, He had such control that they emerged physically unharmed, fully clothed, with not even singed hair or the smell of smoke. They were also emotionally in control—they bore no animosity, no hatred, no desire for revenge. They were at peace.

God insulates worshipers from the fiery physical ordeals we all undergo, but worship also tempers the fiery and potentially damaging thoughts and emotions many of us have: depression, rage, distorted self-image, fear, deep hurt, shame, and hopelessness. It keeps our heart right. God responds to our worship by providing us with direction, confidence, and a desire to live the abundant life He's promised us.

Positions us in high places

In addition to the happy ending of walking out of the furnace unharmed, don't miss the very end of the story. Nebuchadnezzar promoted Shadrach, Meshach and Abednego, and they prospered. I'm sure Nebuchadnezzar believed he was the one who rewarded them, but I'm convinced it was the King of Kings and the Lord of Lords who really caused them to prosper.

I'm sure Shadrach, Meshach, and Abednego didn't get all worked up about another promotion. A higher position in Nebuchadnezzar's kingdom wasn't what they were living for. Similarly, as we worship God, we're brought into His presence and see Him more clearly as the King He is. Eventually we realize that He has made us "a chosen people, a royal priesthood, a holy nation, God's special possession" (1 Peter 2:9, NIV).

You establish a relationship with the Lord of the universe when you repent of your sins and receive His forgiveness and salvation. And, in a sense, that relationship is like any other: how far it develops depends on you. It's up to us if we want to get close to someone, or if we'd rather keep that person at a distance. It's the same with God. If you want your relationship with God to continue to develop—to get closer and closer to Him—the only way to do that is through worship. Lots of people want to keep Him at a "safe" distance (as if that's possible), but as Bob Dylan reminded us, "You gotta serve somebody." If you're not worshiping God, something or somebody else will be your object of worship. But if it's Christ you're worshiping, there's no limit to how far your relationship can go.

Worship is the starting point of discovering the life God intends for you. A. W. Tozer called worship "the missing jewel of evangelism." He wrote: "We're here to be worshipers first and workers only second. We take a convert and immediately make a worker out of him. God never meant it to be so. God meant that a convert should learn to be a worshiper, and after that he can learn to be a worker. . . . The work done by a worshiper will have eternity in it."[4]

What kind of worshiper are you? Are you passionate or reluctant? Consistent or sporadic? On fire for God or lukewarm? Wherever you are in your growing relationship with God, you can always improve. I want to go deeper. I want to experience more of God's presence and become more focused on Him.

---

4 A. W. Tozer, *Tozer on the Holy Spirit* (Deerfield: Moody Press, 2015), p. 8.

CHAPTER 10

MAKE SURE YOU FINISH BEFORE YOU QUIT

We all like an exciting finish, a buzzer-beater game, a Hail Mary pass, or a thrilling plot twist at the end of a movie. Years ago, I was scheduled to minister in Los Angeles, and it just happened to be the year of our youngest son, Jackson's, thirteenth birthday. Two things you need to know about Jackson. One, he's a huge Laker's fan—we have no idea how that happened. Two, he always gets a little shorted because his birthday is two days after Christmas. I thought, *Wouldn't it be awesome if the Lakers were playing at the Staples Center while I'm in California on what also happens to be the kids' Spring Break week!*

Low and behold, they were. And we scored tickets. And Jackson's favorite player, Kobe Bryant, was playing. And it just happened to be one of the greatest athletic events I've ever witnessed. In a game against the Toronto Raptors, Kobe hit a three pointer with five seconds left in regulation to tie the game, then Kobe dunked the go-ahead basket with ten seconds left in overtime. And the crowd went wild . . . and so did the Champions. It took a big sacrifice to get to that game, but what a payoff! When we heard the devastating news of Kobe's untimely death, we reminisced about how special that night was, and how thankful we were to have had that experience.

Elite athletes like Kobe understand how to play 'til the end. They aren't just good starters; they're good finishers. The ebbs and flows of a game are just a condensed version of the ebbs and flows of life except life impacts more than a game. It impacts us personally, the people around us, and the generations to come.

‖‖

WE GET PARALYZED. OR, WE GET ENERGIZED.

‖‖

There's an epidemic of quitting in the world today. Quitting on marriage, quitting on jobs, sometimes tragically, quitting on one's own life. It corresponds to another prevailing problem. We have an epidemic of limited perspective. In an instant-gratification mindset, struggling for more than a day or a season, can lead to overwhelming thoughts that this is all it will ever be. *This is as good as my life will ever get.*

Can you continue to do what you do while tired and discouraged? Can you press forward when it's difficult? Are you going to keep going? And can you continue to face forward though fatigued? When facing the things we have faced over the last few years, there are two choices: We get paralyzed. Or, we get energized.

I was recently on a training call with a few pastors and Dr. Henry Cloud, who is a bestselling author and well-known psychologist. In one of his books he writes of the problem of what educator and psychologist Martin Seligman has termed "learned helplessness":

> *In a learned-helplessness model, the brain begins to interpret events in a negative way, thus reinforcing its belief that "all is bad." For instance, when someone doesn't get a sale, it means "I am a loser, the whole business is bad, and it isn't going to change." These are called the three P's. Events are processed in predictable, negative ways: first, as personalized (I am a bad salesperson); second, as pervasive (everything I do, or every aspect of the business, is bad); and third, as permanent (nothing is going to change). You can easily see why this leads to helplessness and inactivity or paralysis.[5]*

But productive people do not think in a learned-helplessness way. Their internal software is more optimistic, seeing a "non-sale" as just one more number to get past to get to the one who is going to buy and sustaining other such optimistic-thinking paradigms.

Besides the negative thinking of the three Ps in the learned-helplessness model, I also saw a troubling pattern in some individuals—*an even deeper sense of loss of control over things that were, in fact, still in their control.* When someone with this vulnerability is put in a position where things that they cannot control, such as the economy, are affecting them, they shut down and do not execute *in the activities that they can control.*

GETTING THE WHOLE JOB DONE

In Judges 6, God needed to get something done, and He didn't want a quitter. Gideon appears to be a strange choice for God to select as a

---

5 Dr. Henry Cloud, *Necessary Endings* (New York, Harper Business, 2010), p. 56.

national leader. In his own words, "My family is the least in Manasseh, and I am the youngest in my father's house" (v. 15). But the Lord saw Gideon's potential and addressed him as a "valiant warrior" (v. 12). After a couple of initial tests, God gave Gideon his biggest challenge: defeat the powerful Midianites.

Judges 7 shows Gideon with an army of thirty-two thousand men, but God wanted the nation to see that He was responsible for the victory, not the army, so Gideon said that all the soldiers who were scared could go home. Immediately, twenty-two thousand of them deserted.

God said the remaining ten thousand were still too many, so He reduced the army down to three hundred. In the initial confrontation, God confused the Midianites, so that they began to kill one another, and the survivors began to flee. Gideon then summoned all his soldiers to give pursuit, and they began to capture or kill all the enemy leaders. Oh, what can be done with three hundred or one with God!

Whether you are a business leader, a church planter, a sales person, or someone who looks at financial statements, we have probably experienced times when the number of resources (human or financial) don't match the job. We have first-hand experience with the growth charts going in the wrong direction.

The second location we occupied as a church was in a hotel conference center. Little did we know when we signed that lease, that there were three other church plants meeting there on Sundays as well, all sharing the same lobby, with our "auditoriums" sharing the same paper-thin partitions. Many a day, my poignant closing moments of the service would be interrupted by an obnoxious drum solo by the next church over, but I digress. The worst and best day of Celebration Church happened there within a one-week span of time. A man who was part of our launch team approached me and said he "felt led" to sing a solo that Sunday, and admitted that he couldn't carry a tune, but said he was going to be obedient to God, and bless us with a song. I said we couldn't fit it in the schedule that morning, and offered him time to sing on a Wednesday night (where we had twelve people in attendance). He reminded me that his wife was the keyboardist and that they owned the keyboard, and within minutes of my not compromising the schedule, they were on their way out the door, keyboard in hand. I wish they'd just exited the building, but remember, they had an audience of three other churches entering the same lobby, and they made sure they loudly voiced their complaints about our church. I felt a little like Gideon that day, because a couple other families left too, and we didn't have many to start with. But it doesn't end there, the very next week, in walked more guests than we'd had in the whole year before. It was as though God had to clean some things out before He could add some new life. The new people are some of our closest friends and most committed members to this day. I'm so thankful we didn't quit the day the keyboard and crew walked out.

We all have days we want to quit. Gideon and his three hundred men came to the Jordan River. After all that fighting, running up and down mountains, worn out, weary and dead tired, they must have thought, *This looks like a good place to quit. Do we stop here? Or do we cross over and keep going?* He was exhausted, yet the job wasn't over. Your job isn't over either.

■ There are days you feel ill-equipped.

Our children's "classroom" dividers were a homemade rig of sheets and PVC pipes stuck in planters filled with concrete. That was one of many makeshift creations. There were so many weekends that we set up chairs and children's ministry equipment, set out signs . . . it felt so pitiful, small, and insignificant.

I opened my Bible and read: "I *would have lost heart,* unless I had believed that I would see the goodness of the LORD IN THE LAND OF THE LIVING" (Psalm 27:13, NKJV). I remember quoting this verse and saying, "We're living in the land of lack! But we believe that someday it will be the land of the living!"

⎯⎯⎯⎯⎯⎯⎯⎯⎯⎯⎯⎯⎯⎯⎯⎯⎯⎯⎯⎯⎯⎯⎯⎯⎯⎯⎯⎯⎯⎯⎯⎯⎯⎯

SOME SUCCESSES CAN'T BE COUNTED.

⎯⎯⎯⎯⎯⎯⎯⎯⎯⎯⎯⎯⎯⎯⎯⎯⎯⎯⎯⎯⎯⎯⎯⎯⎯⎯⎯⎯⎯⎯⎯⎯⎯⎯

■ There are days you'll feel small.

When the Israelites sent spies into the Promised Land, where God had called them, after God had miraculously brought them from Egypt, parted the Red Sea, and provided food from heaven in the desert . . . after all of that, ten of the twelve spies said, "There we saw the giants [the descendants of Anak came from the giants]; and we were like grasshoppers in our own sight, and so we were in their sight" (Numbers 13:33, NKJV).

We have to keep seeing a future, by faith. That will keep you going. Even though we had far fewer people than we expected, we felt like we were pleasing the Lord. Some successes can't be counted. "Don't despise these small beginnings" (Zechariah 4:10, NLT).

■ There are days when you feel like you can't keep up.

I'll never forget a football practice where the coach had us do the "Train Sprints," which was a post-practice drill (aka: TORTURE), where the team would run in a single-file line around the field. When the coach blew his whistle, the last player running had to sprint and catch up to the first player and the cycle would repeat. When it was my turn to sprint, I was so tired that my pants had fallen below my knees, and I kept tripping on them, but my coach wouldn't let me quit until I finished. Sometimes, you can't keep up and sometimes you can't keep your pants up, but still, don't give up!

■ There are days you won't want to grow (in order to go!)

We eventually grew out of the growing pains of the early days of planting the dream God placed in our hearts. Today, when people ask if we are living the dream that God gave us, my answer is, "No, we never dreamed this big!" God has done above and beyond what we ever could have imagined. But, we had to and continue to have to handle the seasons of exhaustion, disappointment, and delays. We have to keep our focus on Christ's purpose for our lives rather than our own personal success. That's not just because we are in vocational ministry, that's for every person, in whatever calling you are walking in. The work in us was and is as important as the work around us. Paul reminds us, "And let us not grow weary of doing good, for in due season we will reap, if we do not give up" (Galatians 6:9, ESV).

He also wrote, "I have been crucified with Christ; and it is no longer I who live, but Christ lives in me; and the life which now I live in the flesh I live by faith in the Son of God, who loved me and gave Himself up for me" (Galatians 2:20, NASB). Did Paul practice what he preached? Most certainly! While following Jesus' call for his life, he had endured stoning, beatings too numerous to count, whippings, poverty, exposure to the elements, shipwrecks, mental anguish over the problems in the churches he had started, and more (see 2 Corinthians 11:23-29). Yet at the end of his life, he could say with confidence, "I have fought the good fight, I have finished the course, I have kept the faith" (2 Timothy 4:7, NASB). Paul was a finisher, and so are you!

There will be times when you are tempted to compromise. There will be times when you want to quit, but you're not led by your emotions or circumstances anymore. Jesus referred to it as taking up your cross and denying yourself (see Luke 9:23). All day. Every day.

ONE LAST REMINDER

As I wind down the final chapter of this book, I want to leave you with one more plea to apply the things you've been learning along the way. It's not that I'm attempting to "save the best for last." I've honestly been giving you my best insights throughout this book, and I want to close with six challenges for you to take with you and continue to think about. I want us all to finish strong, as we continue to confront compromise.

1) Refuse to compromise in that Jesus is the only Lord and Savior.

Recently, a celebrity that Lori and I love to watch on TV made national news when he released a video of himself at an Islamic mosque for prayer, offering the following explanation: "There's no one way to Heaven, no one way to paradise. It's like a television, now there's over 800 channels on cable, and they're all pretty entertaining. So I'm pretty sure that to get to Heaven, there's got to be more than one route. Because somebody watching another channel or taking another channel than you, they're still getting entertained, and they probably still getting to Heaven."[6]

We were shocked, because he has proclaimed to be a Christ-follower in the past. As much as we enjoy him as an entertainer, he *is not* a theologian, and his opinion is dead wrong. How can I be so sure? Because what he says directly contradicts Jesus. That's one point Jesus wanted to make as He was preparing to finish His time on earth as a human being:

> *"Do not let your heart be troubled; believe in God, believe also in Me.*
> *In My Father's house are many rooms; if that were not so, I would*
> *have told you, because I am going there to prepare a place for you.*
> *And if I go and prepare a place for you, I am coming again and will*
> *take you to Myself, so that where I am, there you also will be. And*
> *you know the way where I am going." Thomas said to Him, "Lord,*
> *we do not know where You are going; how do we know the way?"*
> *Jesus said to him, "I am the way, and the truth, and the life; no one*
> *comes to the Father except through Me." —John 14:1-6 (NASB)*

Jesus had already tried to explain who He was, and He couldn't have stated it any more clearly: "I and the Father are one" (John 10:30, NIV). Here, as He's preparing to die, He's trying to get His dense disciples to comprehend who He really is. And to make things perfectly clear, He didn't say, "I am *a* way and *a* truth." He told them, "I am *the* way, and *the* truth, and *the* life. Without Me, nobody gets to God the Father."

I understand that one of the most offensive statements you can make in our society is to say that Jesus is the only way to God and that other religions are wrong. I don't enjoy arguing with people. I would love to

---

6 Jeannie Ortega Law, "Steve Harvey Says, 'There's No One Way to Heaven,'" *Christian Post*, Jan. 29, 2021, https://www.christianpost.com/news/steve-harvey-says-theres-no-one-way-to-heaven.html

say, "Heaven's big enough for all of us, as long as you're sincere about what you believe," but it just doesn't work that way. I'm not willing to deny God's truth to keep from offending someone. That's why Paul emphasized the importance of public profession:

> *If you confess with your mouth Jesus as Lord, and believe in your heart that God raised Him from the dead, you will be saved; for with the heart a person believes, resulting in righteousness, and with the mouth he confesses, resulting in salvation. For the Scripture says, "Whoever believes in Him will not be put to shame."*
> *—Romans 10:9-11(NASB)*

I fear we're already compromising this truth in many of our churches today, all to keep from appearing intolerant. But now, more than ever, we need to work to finish the ministry that Jesus has given His church. If the church can't uphold the truth that Jesus is our only Lord and Savior, what hope is there for the world?

THE CHURCH SHOULD BE THE CLOSEST PEOPLE CAN GET TO HEAVEN ON EARTH.

2) Refuse to compromise loving the church as Christ loved the church.

These days we're beginning to see more and more animosity toward the church, more mocking from culture. But let me be clear: I'm talking about the church universal—God's body, the group comprised of all people who have genuinely put their faith in Christ and have committed to live for Him. The problem is that if someone doesn't want to be so totally committed to Christ's body, they can find "churches" where they can live by their own rules. It may not be God's church, but it's a church. Some people today shop for churches like ordering a pizza.

I've been a pastor for more than three decades, and I can tell you that there is no perfect church, because churches are filled with imperfect people. People have confided in me saying, "I've been hurt in the church." I'll respond, "Would you like to see my scars?" Some of my greatest hurts have come from people in church. Yet, some of the greatest healing of my hurts has come from the church.

||||||||||||||||||||||||||||||||||||||||||||||||||||||||||||||||||||||||||||||||||||||||||||||||||||||||||||||||||||||||

IT'S IMPOSSIBLE TO LIVE AN EFFECTIVE CHRISTIAN LIFE ALONE.

||||||||||||||||||||||||||||||||||||||||||||||||||||||||||||||||||||||||||||||||||||||||||||||||||||||||||||||||||||||||

Jesus' command to "love one another" (see John 13:34-35) should begin in the church before we try to get out and love the world. When Jesus tells us to pray, "Your will be done, on earth as it is in heaven" (Matthew 6:10, NIV), it has to start in the church. The church should be the closest people can get to heaven on earth. Paul wrote to the church in Ephesus:

> Husbands, love your wives, just as Christ also loved the church and gave Himself up for her, so that He might sanctify her, having cleansed her by the washing of water with the word, that He might present to Himself the church in all her glory, having no spot or

wrinkle or any such things; but that she would be holy and blameless.
—*Ephesians 5:25-27 (NASB)*

It's impossible to live an effective Christian life alone. You can't finish what you start if you're unable to connect God's love to other people. I hear people say, "I can be a Christian without going to church." There

EXTENDED ISOLATION MAKES US VULNERABLE.

is absolutely nothing to support that biblically. The New Testament knows nothing of a churchless Christianity. When we are converted to Christ, we become part of His family—the church. Besides, extended isolation makes us vulnerable. Pirates attack solo ships, not armadas. Prowling lions attack stragglers in the herd. You've heard, "There's strength in numbers," and there's unlimited strength in numbers of people who come together to support one another while following Christ. Jesus said, "I will build My church; and the gates of Hades will not overpower it" (Matthew 16:18, NASB). You might not like the church right now, but you'd better learn to love it. You need it, and you won't finish without it.

3) Refuse to compromise what God thinks about sin.

Jesus didn't come down from heaven and die to set you free *to* sin. He died to keep you free *from* sin. Some people learn about that wonderful doctrine of grace and think, *Wow. Now I can do anything I want!* Certainly, God can forgive anything, but that doesn't mean we should try to set new sin records! Paul tried to make this point as he wrote Romans:

> *What shall we say then? Are we to continue in sin so that grace*
> *may increase? Far from it! How shall we who died to sin still live*
> *in it? Or do you not know that all of us who have been baptized into*
> *Christ Jesus have been baptized into His death? Therefore we have*
> *been buried with Him through baptism into death, so that, just as*
> *Christ was raised from the dead through the glory of the Father, so*
> *we too may walk in newness of life. For if we have become united*
> *with Him in the likeness of His death, certainly we shall also be*
> *in the likeness of His resurrection, knowing this, that our old self*
> *was crucified with Him, in order that our body of sin might be done*
> *away with, so that we would no longer be slaves to sin. —Romans*
> *6:1-6 (NASB)*

Christ has set you free from sin. He has elevated you to "newness of life." So now, what are you going to do? If you've truly died to sin and self, you'll understand that God's grace is one of the greatest gifts He can impart, and you'll be so thankful that your sinful life will no longer be appealing. However, some people misunderstand grace and take it

WE MUST NEVER TAKE GRACE FOR GRANTED.

for granted. Dietrich Bonhoeffer wrote about "cheap grace," defined as the preaching of forgiveness without repentance, baptism without church discipline, and grace without the cross, without discipleship, without Jesus Christ. We must never take grace for granted.

Even worse, however, are those who abuse grace purposefully. Jude wrote about such people: "For certain people have crept in [to the church] unnoticed, those who were long beforehand marked out for this condemnation, ungodly persons who turn the grace of our God into indecent behavior and deny our only Master and Lord, Jesus Christ" (Jude 1:4, NASB). I hear people speculating about the signs of the end times, and they ask for my opinion. I tell them to stop worrying about heavenly signs (moons and clouds and such), or for secret codes within Scripture. I point them to this verse in Jude.

4) Refuse to compromise about true salvation.

I have no qualms about the "sinner's prayer"—something along the lines of, "Dear Jesus, I'm a sinner. I believe You died for me on the cross, so my sins would be forgiven. I receive you as my Lord and Savior. Thank You for coming into my life. Amen."

||||||||||||||||||||||||||||||||||||||||||||||||||||||||||||||||||||||||||||||||||||||||||||||||||||||||||||||||

IF YOU DON'T READ YOUR BIBLE, YOU DON'T HAVE A MORAL STANDARD TO LIVE BY.

||||||||||||||||||||||||||||||||||||||||||||||||||||||||||||||||||||||||||||||||||||||||||||||||||||||||||||||||

However, I become very concerned when some people treat this prayer as an end rather than the beginning of their relationship with God. It's as if some people, from that point, think, *Now that I've said the magic words, I'm in. Now I can do whatever I want.* But living for Christ involves so much more than a one-time prayer.

Jesus warns us that salvation should never be considered lightly. He says, "The gate is wide and the way is broad that leads to destruction, and there are many who enter through it. For the gate is narrow and the way is constricted that leads to life, and there are few who find it" (Matthew 7:13-14, NASB).

As Jesus prayed for His disciples, He defined genuine salvation: "And this is eternal life, that they may know You, the only true God, and Jesus Christ whom You have sent" (John 17:3, NASB).

5) Refuse to compromise the truth of Scripture.

Believers should always hold their Bibles in high regard. If you don't read your Bible, you don't have a moral standard to live by. We live in a progressive society that tends to drift further and further from God's truth, and Scripture doesn't endorse many of the beliefs of our "enlightened" culture. The Bible isn't always politically correct. In ten or twenty years, our culture will likely have a completely different standard from its current one. But do you know what? The Word of God will be just as reliable and unchanging as it ever was.

Isaiah tells us, "The grass withers, the flower fades, but the word of our God will stand forever" (Isaiah 40:8, ESV). People come and go. Most are quickly forgotten. But God's Word is eternal. It's not good enough to be good enough. We must live our lives according to the Bible because "All Scripture is inspired by God and beneficial for teaching, for rebuke, for correction, for training in righteousness; so that the man or woman of God may be fully capable, equipped for every good work" (2 Timothy 3:16-17, NASB).

I believe the reason our country has been so blessed in the past is because it was founded on the truth of God's Word. And I think the reason we've had so many problems lately is that we're straying further away from His truth. It's time to stop trying to compromise with the world. God's Word is truth, and truth cannot be compromised.

6) Refuse to compromise your trust in the power of the Holy Spirit.

In Jesus' final days on earth, He wanted to assure His disciples that He would never leave them helpless. At the time, they couldn't comprehend what He was trying to tell them, but afterward, it all made sense:

> *"I tell you the truth: it is to your advantage that I am leaving; for if I do not leave, the Helper will not come to you; but if I go, I will send Him to you. And He, when He comes, will convict the world regarding sin, and righteousness, and judgment: regarding sin, because they do not believe in Me; and regarding righteousness, because I am going to the Father and you no longer are going to see Me; and regarding judgment, because the ruler of this world has been judged." —John 16:7-11 (NASB)*

Jesus knew His disciples were feeling helpless and vulnerable. All His talk of dying and leaving surely made them fearful because He would no longer be there to comfort and direct them. Yes, He was about to return to God, but He would send the Holy Spirit—a Helper—in His place. After Jesus' resurrection, He gave His followers more specific instructions:

> *Gathering them together, He commanded them not to leave Jerusalem, but to wait for what the Father had promised, "Which," He said, "you heard of from Me; for John baptized with water, but you will be baptized with the Holy Spirit not many days from now." So, when they had come together, they began asking Him, saying, "Lord, is it at this time that You are restoring the kingdom to Israel?" But He said to them, "It is not for you to know periods of time or appointed times which the Father has set by His own authority; but you will*

receive power when the Holy Spirit has come upon you; and you shall
be My witnesses both in Jerusalem and in all Judea, and Samaria,
and as far as the remotest part of the earth." —*Acts 1:4-8 (NASB)*

Jesus' ministry had been limited to the people able to see Him, hear Him, and be healed by Him. His followers were about to discover that, through the Holy Spirit, the power of God would indwell all believers, exponentially expanding the influence of their ministry.

They didn't have to wait long. It was only a few days later, on the day of Pentecost, when they received the miraculous gifting of God—being filled with the Holy Spirit. The church began, and then grew quickly because of the Holy Spirit's signs and wondrous power, manifested through God's people.

||||||||||||||||||||||||||||||||||||||||||||||||||||||||||||||||||||||||||||||||||||||||||||||||||||||||||||||||||||||||||||

REMEMBER: THE CHOICE TO CONTINUE IS ALWAYS UP TO YOU.

||||||||||||||||||||||||||||||||||||||||||||||||||||||||||||||||||||||||||||||||||||||||||||||||||||||||||||||||||||||||||||

Believers still need the power of the Holy Spirit if we're going to finish the tasks God gives us to do. We can be sure, however, that God will never give us an assignment without also providing the power for us to complete it.

Keep these things in mind as you go out and live for God in a world that needs to hear the truth about Him. Many people are listening to untruths, half-truths, and theologies based on wishful thinking. They're eager to compromise, so God's people must stand firmly on His truth, never taking the easy way out of a difficult situation. You can expect to go through trying periods of extreme fatigue, uncertainty, crankiness, and worse, but just keep going. Don't think about turning around or looking for shortcuts. Remember: the choice to continue is always up to you. Finish the race. Receive the victor's crown. And one day you'll hear God say, "Well done, good and faithful servant."

ACKNOWLEDGMENTS

Jesus is the reason I have a story to tell. I'm thankful for my salvation and the opportunity to share His *hope* with others.

While this book may contain personal thoughts and stories, it also contains the love and dedication of so many who worked hard to bring it to life.

To Jim and Sara Champion, my memories of you have forever shaped who I am.

To Greg and Keith Champion, you are real champions.

To Mel Davis, thank you for pastoring me. I admire everything about you, and it has been an extraordinary blessing to sit under your leadership.

To Daniel Gonzales, thank you for walking alongside me in the journey to develop this book. I'm even more thankful that you and Celeste have walked with Lori and me for the last twenty years of ministry.

To Christy Ash, thank you for designing the cover of this book and also for being a rock star on our team at Celebration!

To Sam Chand, the AVAIL Team, and Pat Springle, thank you! You brilliantly surrounded me with the best talent and hearts to help bring this book from a dream to a reality.

To my ARC Family and Friends, I am thankful that we do not do ministry alone.

To my Celebration Church family, being your pastor has been the thrill of my life. Let's continue to make Jesus famous!

To those reading this book, God has more for you, and you have more to give God. I pray that you are inspired and challenged. Let's stand for truth no matter what.

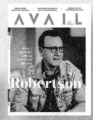

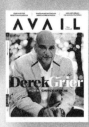

AVAIL +

TRY FOR 30 DAYS *AND RECEIVE*
THE SEQUENCE TO SUCCESS
BUNDLE FREE

$79 VALUE

+ BOOK
+ STUDY GUIDE
+ ONLINE COURSE
+ LIVE CLASS
+ MORE

The Art *of* Leadership

This isn't just another leadership collective...this is the next level of networking, resources, and empowerment designed specifically for leaders like you.

Whether you're an innovator in ministry, business, or your community, **AVAIL +** is designed to take you to your next level. Each one of us needs connection. Each one of us needs practical advice. Each one of us needs inspiration. **AVAIL +** is all about equipping you, so that you can turn around and equip those you lead.

THEARTOFLEADERSHIP.COM/CHAND